D1562881

The Problem
of *Suffering*

A Father's Hope

Revised and Expanded

Gregory P. Schulz

CONCORDIA PUBLISHING HOUSE · SAINT LOUIS

Published by Concordia Publishing House
3558 S. Jefferson Ave., St. Louis, MO 63118-3968
1-800-325-3040 • www.cph.org

Manufactured in the United States of America

Library of Congress Cataloging-in-Publication Data

Schulz, Gregory.
  The problem of suffering : a father's hope / Gregory P. Schulz. -- 2nd, expanded ed.
    p. cm.
  Includes bibliographical references (p.   ).
  ISBN 978-0-7586-2661-5
1. Children--Death--Religious aspects--Christianity. 2. Suffering--Religious aspects--Christianity.
3. Schulz, Gregory. 4. Consolation. I. Title.

  BV4907.S45 2011
  248.8'66--dc23

                                2011026259

1   2   3   4   5   6   7   8   9   10   20   19   18   17   16   15   14   13   12   11

For Paula,
beloved wife and loving mother.

For Kara and Daniel,
loving sister and brother to Kyleigh
and Stephan.

On the foundation of His promise
for us all:

"I will turn their mourning into joy"

(Jeremiah 31:13*)*

Contents

Foreword

WARNING: After you've read this book you'll never be the same again. You will be challenged by its intellectual depth, encouraged by its spiritual consolation, and blown away by its honesty. Like a roller-coaster, it will lift you to dizzying heights of insight, plunge you down into the deepest imaginable human pain, then lift you out again into hope.

Pain and suffering come in different sizes and intensities for different people, but they come inevitably to us all. A lot of ink has been spilled over the centuries on the so-called "problem of evil," but there's not much help in that. Anyone who has personally experienced the mind-numbing and gut-wrenching impact of suffering, pain, or loss can tell you the last thing anyone needs in the midst of that mess is intellectual reflection and explanation. What you need is the honest truth. And such honesty is rarely pleasant.

Gregory Schulz is a first-rate philosopher and academician. He is also a pastor and a teacher with decades of experience in parish ministry and both secondary and post-secondary education. But first and foremost, he's a husband and a father. Greg the philosopher will stimulate your mind, Greg the pastor will strengthen your soul, but Greg the father will grip your heart. Woven throughout this remarkable little book is the heartbreaking story of the suffering and death of two of the Schulz' four children, victims of rare and debilitating diseases.

Greg pulls no punches and minces no words; he portrays a father's pain in all its bitter reality. Not only does he open his remarkable mind to his readers, but he dares to open his hurting soul as well. And we are all the richer for it. Using language reminiscent of C. S. Lewis's *A Grief Observed*, the personal chronicle of the Oxford don's raw anguish at his wife's death, Dr. Schulz lays bare the unthinkable torment and wrenching loss he and his wife, Paula, experienced during the lingering illnesses and subsequent deaths of their baby girl Kyleigh and their adolescent son Stephan.

During the years I was privileged to teach pastoral theology at Concordia Theological Seminary I used the earlier edition of this book to teach fledgling pastors the art of caring for suffering souls. It was a transformational experience for my students, many of whom were themselves fathers of young children. Greg's vivid narrative put a face on human suffering, to be sure, but it also placed his personal horror squarely into the larger context of God's own suffering Son and His healing love.

Martin Luther, himself no stranger to suffering and pain, once wrote, "A theologian of glory calls evil good and good evil. A theologian of the cross calls the thing what it actually is."[1] God's love, you see, is revealed most vividly in the bitter suffering and horrific death of His incarnate Son, Jesus Christ. Christians needn't camouflage grief or paint smiley faces on human suffering; we take our reality straight. In the light of Christ's cross we can discover God at work in the very midst of suffering.

Greg's premise is that grieving people don't ever "get over" their grief. It is, rather, their God-given *task* to *grieve* and to *mourn*. Christian or not, grieving people all mourn the loss of their loved ones. Grief is the experience of the absence of those we love. In this remarkable book Gregory Schulz ably serves us all as companion in our grief. He knows intimately well the severe mercy of God hidden under grief and tears. He teaches us how to grieve in hope— with quiet confidence in the One who Himself was raised from the dead and now lives forever in triumphant glory.

Harold L. Senkbeil, MDiv, STM, DD
Waukesha, Wisconsin

Preface

In his 1940 book *The Problem of Pain*, C. S. Lewis explained that he was writing "to solve an intellectual problem raised by suffering," but that people in pain need "the least tincture of the love of God" more than anything.[1]

There are many of us who hunger and thirst for God's love while we watch our children suffer and die. In the middle of days spent at bedsides in intensive care units and during dreary nights spent monitoring temperatures and blood counts, we need a tincture of God's love more than anything. In my first congregation I regularly visited a shut-in church member whose throat had been so ravaged by disease that she could not tolerate even a swallow of wine. For Holy Communion I would break off a tiny wafer and dip it into the Communion wine so that she could receive her Lord's body and blood by *tincture*.

Lewis wrote as if the problem of pain can be solved intellectually, as if we can acquire equilibrium by thinking about suffering in a certain way. I have learned from Job, from St. Paul, and from the father of Magdalena Luther (who died at age 13), that I cannot by my own reason or strength believe in my Lord or come to Him. More, I cannot find a satisfactory intellectual answer for the suffering and pain my children have been through. As a Lutheran pastor and theologian of the cross, I know that my responsibility is to preach Christ crucified, not suffering justified. As a philosopher, I recognize the obscenity of arguing by means of calculations of consequences or instrumentality that the pain of others can be explained. As a parent of children who have suffered and suffered before their deaths, I know that there is no equilibrium to be had this side of heaven.

The Lord has been my tutor for this problem of evil, as philosophers call it. His curriculum is what one widower called "a severe mercy." To be honest with you, there have been months when the *last* thing I wanted was to be anywhere near the Lord, my God, much less to listen for an explanation for the agony wracking the little soul being held on my lap, or for the torment being visited on my dear wife and other children.

I anticipate more days and nights of suffering until He lifts me out of this valley of tears. I am very tired, undeniably weak. My presence in the green pastures of heaven will have to be all His doing, as is my presence in His church today. This is what we believers have learned from Holy Scripture to call *grace*. Grace is what we taste in the tincture of God's love.

For a decade and a half I was witness to the pain my Jesus inflicted on my older son through a complicated chronic autoimmune disease. I also witnessed His hand on my youngest daughter, a lovely little girl who died five days before her first birthday following a year of surgeries, seizures, and infections. I wrote the first four chapters of this little book while the earth was settling over Kyleigh's tiny grave. The last two chapters I wrote a number of years later. Now it is time to send this to you.

This book you are holding will never share Lewis's purpose of providing an intellectually satisfying answer for pain. It is not meant for that. When those that we love, and especially our children, are suffering and dying, what answer can there be? As long as we live in this life, this great tribulation, there can be no closure to our grief. In place of a comprehensive, intellectual answer, this book is meant to bring a tincture of God's love for us in our suffering. From that little taste, we may go on to enjoy a rich measure of His mercy, pressed down and overflowing.

These chapters come from one soul to another. From a parent to a parent. From someone else's father to you in your suffering. From one sufferer to another. They come from God's unending Word to our everyday world. Together, let us endure awhile longer. Let us "taste and see that the LORD is good" (Psalm 34:8).

"Blessed be the God and Father of our Lord Jesus Christ, the Father of mercies and God of all comfort, who comforts us in all our affliction, so that we may be able to comfort those who are in any affliction, with the comfort with which we ourselves are comforted by God." (2 Corinthians 1:3–4)

Gregory P. Schulz

Please note, for a fuller discussion and Bible study of suffering and Luther's theology of the cross, and for an annotated bibliography, see *The Problem of Suffering: A Companion Study Guide and Resources for Pastors and Christian Caregivers*, also from CPH.

Acknowledgments

Thank you to Harold Senkbeil, as well as to the sainted Donald Deffner, mentors and friends in Christ who encouraged me to write and to expand my story. To Kara Schulz-Pierce and to Ib Van Meyer who loaned their strong words to the Epilogue, to Dianne Koser for typing portions of my manuscript, and to Scot Kinnaman, my thoughtful and compassionate editor, for bringing this expanded edition to print, my thanks as well.

CHAPTER 1

Call Me Job

"Weeping is preferred to working and suffering exceeds all doing."

—Martin Luther,
"Seven Penitential Psalms"[1]

One step off the blacktop road, a moment spent balancing on the concrete curb, and I am standing ankle deep in snow. The sun is warm for the first day of Wisconsin winter, warm enough this morning that, without brushing away the snow, I can see her name just above mine, written in bronze, down at my feet.

The melting snow for contrast. An inch of pink-grained marble for a frame. Bronze roses as a matte. Here is my name, inscribed as part of hers: Kyleigh Honor-Lillie Schulz April 26, 1992—April 21, 1993.

Even in the season when the snow melts, my little girl will be hidden. Let me show you where. Westward just a bit. Measure it out, foot by foot. From the top of the marker, at the bronze roses, heel to toe. There, that small depression in the grass shows the place. There is where we sowed the curly-headed seed twenty months ago.

Kyleigh is hidden. For the second Christmas I have come here to play hide-and-seek. The rules? God hides her; I seek.

The wire tripod pushes easily into the thawing ground. This year's wreath is as evergreen as a father can make it—artificial greenery with pink bows and shiny Christmas ornaments wired onto it. Last year's wreath withered brown by mid-January; this year's will be green for as long as I want.

Intending to stand in the snow, I am a penitent, weary of life, praying in this season of Advent for God's second advent to come quickly, quickly. But the day is unexpectedly warm and comfortable. The God of hide-and-seek reminds me of His words, evergreen, everlasting, and alive: "Set your minds on things that are above, where Christ is, seated at the right hand of God. Set your minds on things that are above, not on things that are on earth. For you have died, and your life is hidden with Christ in God. When Christ, who is your life appears, then you also will appear with Him in glory" (Colossians 3:2–4). This is a text that I usually preach at Easter, the season for hiding and seeking and appearing, but here at my daughter's grave, I certainly do not feel like a preacher, but like the father of an abducted little girl.

So the Christmas wreath commemorates our cemetery celebration. I will proclaim glad tidings of great joy for all the people from the pulpit. But first, Merry Christmas, Kyleigh. Are you singing the same carols we sing this week? What child is this, laid to rest?

My Kyleigh is hidden. Hidden, not by snow nor grass nor earth, but by the hand of God Himself. Hidden by the hidden God who made my little girl suffer and die.

The Shout of No!

Let us sit upon the ground and tell sad tales of suffering: my daughter's, my son's, yours. What exactly is suffering? As Nicholas Wolterstorff lamented the sudden death of his son, Eric, in a mountain climbing accident, he described suffering as a shout of No! He explained that suffering is the shout of No "by nerves and gut and gland and heart to pain, to death," and to injustice and abandonment.[2]

Suffering is not simply being in pain or being sympathetic to those who are in pain. It is a complaint, a lament about the wrongness of the pain. Suffering is indeed the shout of No! But it isn't a cry into the void. For us Christians, it is a shout and cry to God. He is God. He is almighty. And yet, look at these great evils in our lives. No, Lord, it isn't right!

Suffering Takes the Shape of Our Children

One geneticist who worked with Kyleigh included the following observations in his lengthy evaluation of her. I offer his diagnosis in order to make my case that Kyleigh's pain was not right. I cannot have it engraved with an iron stylus on rock, but I can inscribe my lament in this book.

> Development has been severely and globally delayed. Kyleigh has never developed social smile and is unable to roll over. . . . This unfortunate young child has several major clinical problems that are difficult to tie neatly together with a single underlying diagnosis. In brief summary, these problems are:
>
> 1. Severe psychomotor retardation with seizure activity and neuropathic posturing.
> 2. Apparently true congenital hypoparathyroidism.
> 3. Keritinization of the corneal epithelium with subsequent sloughing or abrasion.
> 4. Chronic Candidal skin rash.
> 5. Recurrent unexplained fevers.
> 6. Persistent low-grade acidosis.

God did not give her suffering in brief summary. Kyleigh suffered episodes of apnea, when she stopped breathing. She could not suck or swallow and had to have a gastrostomy so that we could feed her directly into the stomach. Her diaphragm had to be surgically augmented. Her eyes, at first sensitive to all light, eventually clouded over with a milky film. At times, a mild sound or a soft touch would send her into a back-arching seizure. There were rashes and fevers and infections. Surgeons installed a central intravenous line into her chest.

Most days, a bath would make her miserable. Though she liked to be held, there were times when even the stimulation of touching her skin made her cry with pain. We never saw Kyleigh smile.

Her Lord expected us to abide by the prayer, "My times are in Your hands, O Lord." Meanwhile, Kyleigh (poor little Kyleigh!) and all of us who loved her and cared for her suffered.

We suffered in the final days of Kyleigh's suffering.

> *Another Monday in the cruelest month. It is early afternoon. Twenty minutes ago I left her hospital room to fetch Kyleigh's brothers and sister. Now that I have pulled Kara, Daniel, and Stephan out of class, I am driving back to the hospital as quickly as possible.*

> *The kids know, but they don't know. Here is a father-to-children speech anyone would dread. I tell them as we pause at a stoplight. "We have to go see Kyleigh right away. She has some very bad infections . . . and the doctors . . . don't think she will live . . . more than a day or two, at most."*
>
> *In the backseat, Kara cries. So do I. Daniel becomes very quiet. Next to me in the front seat, Stephan shouts. "No, Dad! Make them do something! Tell the doctors they have to do something!"*

Stephan knew what he was shouting about. Since birth he has suffered. Open-heart surgery, intestinal scopings, endless biopsies. A Broviac line surgically installed in his heart. A coma. Month-long stays in hospitals. Medicines and restricted diets. The prospect of a liver transplant.

Kyleigh's brothers and sister were right to shout and cry. They were right to scream "No" to God. It wasn't simply that they were hurting, and God, like any other compassionate person, would forgive their outburst. They were right to shout and cry "No" because they knew then in their nerves and in their guts, in their glands and in their hearts, that their little sister's suffering and dying were not right. They know it today, these years after her death. They know that this is not the way life should be.

God knows it too.

A Believer's Question

What we cry out in the midst of all this suffering is a good question, a believer's question: "Why, my God, why?"

There must be a purpose to what has happened, to what is happening to my children. What father can believe that his infant daughter has died for nothing? What parent could accept the thought that his son bravely has to face surgeries and agonies for no reason whatsoever? What can justify such suffering?

Plainly, I have to cry out to my God. Where else can I go?

Job cried out to him. We battered parents always cry out to God. Some four thousand years ago in Uz, perhaps in the days of Abraham, Job suffered. He suffered also for his children, all ten slain in one day. Dust and ashes. Sores and grief. Seven days of silent wondering. Then our question erupted from Job's soul. *Why?!* He cursed his day, the night of his birth (Job 3). "Why wasn't I stillborn?" (Job 3:11). "Or why was I not as a hidden stillborn child, as infants who never see the light?" (Job 3:16). Why be born, just to suffer and prolong the agony? "Why is light given to him who is in misery, and life to the bitter in soul, who long for death, but it comes not?" (Job 3:20–21). Why, Job asked, should God keep him alive in the middle of such agony of body and soul?

Why?

Think about Job's suffering. Think about Job's suffering as he cried out to God. No unbeliever, I think, could have uttered such an indictment of the Lord God. No unbeliever could target his question so precisely or could have felt that it was in actuality the hand of God that weighed so heavily upon him and his loved ones.

Behold, He passes by me, and I see Him not;
    He moves on, but I do not perceive Him.
Behold, He snatches away; who can turn Him back?
    Who will say to Him, 'What are You doing?'
God will not turn back His anger;
    beneath Him bowed the helpers of Rahab.

How then can I answer Him,
    choosing my words with Him?
Though I am in the right, I cannot answer Him;
    I must appeal for mercy to my accuser.
If I summoned Him and He answered me,
    I would not believe that He was listening
    to my voice.
For He crushes me with a tempest
    and multiplies my wounds without cause;
He will not let me get my breath,
    but fills me with bitterness.
If it is a contest of strength, behold, He is mighty!
    If it is a matter of justice, who can summon Him?

Though I am in the right, my own mouth would
condemn me;

    though I am blameless, He would prove me
perverse.

(Job 9:11–20)

Call me Job. I know Job's God, and Job's God knows
me. Job's God is, in fact, a blood relative of mine, my
Kinsman-Redeemer. In Hebrew He is called *goel*, a relative
who has the ability to adopt, to buy, to save me personally.
But, I want to ask Him, is this any way for a Father and
Redeemer to treat His children?

It's not just that I know *about* God, you understand; I know
beyond any doubt who He is. I know that He is the Father, Son,
and Spirit who began my universe in the beginning. I know He
made me, the me writing these words, in the secret place of my
mother's womb. I know that Jesus, the virgin-born, crucified,
and risen Jesus Christ, is God in the flesh. I know God.

I also know what God did to Job, and I know what He
has done to my children. He targeted Job by name; I feel
as though He has targeted me and mine too: "Have you
considered my servant Gregory, his daughter Kyleigh, or his
son Stephan?"

> Let Him take His rod away from me, and let
> not dread of Him terrify me. Then I would
> speak without fear of Him, for I am not so in
> myself. (Job 9:34–35)

This *Why* is something we saints have been praying for centuries in the *How long, O Lord, how long?* of many psalms. There is no essential difference between Job's suffering all those millennia ago and our suffering today. Take up your cross; you are following Job's God.

Cry out "No" with all your heart, soul, and mind. Let us bear in our arms our children, blind and handicapped, afflicted and suffering, to the Lord our God. Let us see whether He will crush us with a tempest.

Or whether He will be our Redeemer.

CHAPTER 2

The Test

"Let us think honestly and speak biblically:
Philosophically speaking, theodicies end in
betrayals and sin against those who suffer;
theologically, we preach Christ crucified, not
suffering justified (see Romans 8, Augsburg
Confession, Article 5)."
— Gregory Schulz[1]

Four months after Kyleigh died, my wife and I bought a puppy. Jazz was a black-white-beige Shetland sheepdog. Bright, eager to please, she brought love and warmth into an empty part of the family circle. She became, I suppose, a surrogate sister to Kara, our older daughter.

> *Two weeks after Jazz entered our household. I am having a dream. A fire giving off "darkness visible." Over the fire a spit, suspended vertically. On the spit a small animal, skinned white and blood-streaked. Jazz, I think.*

Abruptly I wake up—and hurry downstairs, my hand skimming the railing, into the darkness. I go, not to check on the dog, but to our son Stephan's room. It's where I always go when I wake up in the night. To reach my hand to his face to feel his breath or to tousle his hair until he moves. I'm not sure that we parents ever trust the angels' ministry when we are awake. Receive the sign of the cross on the head and heart (and liver), reminding heaven that you have been redeemed and baptized by Christ the crucified.

A quick check on Daniel in his room and Kara in hers and then back to bed. Again the fire, the figure, and the dark. The vertical spit revolves until I can see the face of the creature skewered there.

Her eyes open. For a second, they are the brown eyes of our sheltie puppy. A blink, and they become the milky blue eyes of my infant daughter. I glance to the left and see the man still there. I cannot move or even open my mouth. He watches me calmly. Not a word.

Not a gesture. "Dad?" I start to think. No. Is it my father? "My . . . Wait! . . . Our Father in heaven?!" And I wake up.

What we think during the day, we dream at night. Until writing this down just now, I had never said it aloud, but all along I have felt that God is the one who has been jabbing and prodding and tormenting my children.

In the third month of Kyleigh's first hospital stay, a chaplain sat down with me and asked, "Greg, what's your theodicy about this?" Pastor to pastor, he was using the technical term for what John Milton sets out to do at the start of *Paradise Lost*: "to justify the ways of God to man."[2]

Theodicy, explaining God's justice in the face of suffering, is a pursuit of many Christians. Theodicy is what C. S. Lewis sought to provide with his book *The Problem of Pain*. The well-known apologist says in the preface, "The only purpose of the book is to solve the intellectual problem raised by suffering."[3]

Can this problem be solved intellectually or cognitively? We suffer as whole people, so suffering is not just in our minds. Nicholas Wolterstorff, whose *Lament* I mentioned earlier, concludes, "In the valley of suffering, despair and bitterness are brewed. But there also character is made. The valley of suffering is the vale of soul-making."[4] This is not an adequate answer either. Do we really believe that an infant's soul is being shaped by having her suffer from the evening of her first breath until the night of her last heartbeat?

The answers we come up with remind me of the statistical maxim that numbers are meaningless when applied to an individual. In the case of suffering considered generically or at a distance, we can produce many plausible-sounding ways of justifying the ways of God to man. But when we are talking about the suffering of any given soul, there is no theodicy. Theodicies are meaningless when applied to the individual. Meaningless, meaningless, a vapor.

Think of the children. At bedside during Kyleigh's last hospital stay, one of her regular nurses visited with me about her son who was stillborn. She talked quietly about her grief for other children on the same hospital floor who were suffering. "Do you know," she whispered, "that right now there are four children on the floor who aren't here because of accidents or diseases? They're here because their caregivers got angry and shook them until their brains got swollen and damaged." Can you justify God's inaction?

What about when their pain and suffering cannot be blamed on abusive parents or drunken drivers? What about the diseases that afflict our children? In our children we see suffering distilled to its dregs.

As I look down into the Isolette of my newborn—seizing, back arched, wrinkled hands clenched, unable to catch breath to cry—what does it mean to maintain that she is passing through the valley of soul-making? As I cradle our skinny five-year-old on my lap, what intellectual answer can anyone provide to explain why he should have to endure open-heart surgery, incessant diarrhea, coma, and nights of fevers and sleeplessness?

Suffering is intensely personal. So God's answer to the problem of suffering must be very, very personal indeed.

Kenneth Surin recommends the personal answer to suffering in his essay "Taking Suffering Seriously." He says that we have no other choice but to *wait*. We Christians have to wait for God's revelation about the pain and suffering that exist in His creation. We have to wait for the message of the cross of His Son.[5] We feel like Old Testament folk, waiting and waiting for the Messiah to save our children and us. In fact, though, we are New Testament people, living in the latter days. "Long ago, at many times and in many ways, God spoke to our fathers by the prophets, but in these last days He has spoken to us by His Son" (Hebrews 1:1–2). Jesus is the Person who is the answer to suffering, which is inherently personal.

What God reveals in Jesus is supremely important for us sufferers. There are three matters on which He pulls aside the curtain (that is what "reveal" means in the original language of His Word) to show us sufferers the reality behind appearances.

(1) What is the cause of the suffering?

(2) Who could ever make something good come out of our suffering?

(3) And when will it end?

Heaven itself, God's answer to this last question, I will discuss later.

The Cause of Suffering

The first matter of God's revelation is the most difficult. What is God's answer to the problem of our suffering? We need to know: Who is responsible for suffering, our children's and ours?

God Himself causes our suffering. He is not the cause of sin, mind you, but He is the cause of our suffering.

To His revelation, then. In Romans 8, Paul says,

> For I consider that the sufferings of this present time are not worth comparing with the glory that is to be revealed to us. For the creation waits with eager longing for the revealing of the sons of God. For the creation was subjected to futility, not willingly, but because of Him who subjected it, in hope that the creation itself will be set free from its bondage to corruption and obtain the freedom of the glory of the children of God. For we know that the whole creation has been groaning together in the pains of childbirth until now. And not only the creation, but we ourselves, who have the firstfruits of the Spirit, groan inwardly as we wait eagerly for adoption as sons, the redemption of our bodies. For in this hope we were saved. Now hope that is seen is not hope. For who hopes for what he

> sees? But if we hope for what we do not see,
> we wait for it with patience. (Romans 8:18–25)

Cells malform and organs wear themselves out not by chance, but rather by divine decree. In the tried and true language of the old theologians, suffering is *accident*, something added to our lives, not something originally created into it. Added, according to the apostolic word, by God Himself, "who subjected it, in hope that the creation itself will be set free from its bondage to corruption" (Romans 8:20–21). Suffering is a method of hope on God's part.

Sin and death are the wages of Adam's sin and mine. But suffering, the *No* that I scream as I see my children's pain, this is a gift from my Father. It is a gift to teach me that our pains have purpose and meaning. I am having labor pains.

In expounding Psalm 6, Luther reminds us his pastoral and practical way to remember, first and foremost, that our suffering comes from the Almighty.

> First. In all trials and affliction man should first of all run to God; he should realize and accept the fact that everything is sent by God, whether it comes from the devil or from man. This is what the prophet does here. In this psalm [Psalm 6] he mentions his trials, but first he hurries to God and accepts these trials from Him; for this is the way to learn patience

and the fear of God. But he who looks to man
and does not accept these things from God
becomes impatient and a despiser of God.[6]

It seems strange (even blasphemous, I know) to hold that
God brings suffering into our world and into the lives of our
children. But it is so. After chronicling Job's grief, the Holy
Spirit tells us that our brother was comforted "for all the evil
that *the LORD had brought upon him*" (Job 42:11, italics added).

My fellow pastors try to help by explaining, "God
doesn't *want* your children to suffer. It's better to say that He
allowed this to happen." But as Luther and Psalm 6 teach us,
this, too, is from God. God's permissive will is still God's will.

strange or unfamiliar

This is a very painful example of what we Lutherans call
the *alien work* of God the Holy Spirit. His main and favorite
work is to comfort us with the Good News of what the Son
has done for us with His own death and resurrection. His
main work is to bring us to heaven to live with Him there.
But before we will become interested at all in trusting Jesus
to be our Way, He has to show us beyond all doubt how lost
we and our families are. This is the first unit in the lesson of
suffering. And it is terrifying.

The Cause of Death

There is nothing more terrifying than seeing the wages of
sin present in your own child. The terror lies in knowing (and

34

I do mean "knowing" in the Hebrew sense of understanding by hands-on experience) that I as a father am the medium for the sin that brings my child's death. When that chaplain at Children's Hospital asked me about my theodicy, all I could tell him was, "I certainly know how real my sin is."

Consider how God terrifies a father with the reality of sin as expressed in the obsolete sacrament of circumcision. In a New Year's Day sermon drawn from Luke 2:21 ("And at the end of eight days, when he was circumcised, he was called Jesus, the name given by the angel before he was conceived in the womb"), Luther preached,

> God was not concerned about the circumcision, but about the humiliation of proud nature and reason.
>
> God has here taught every one that nobody can become righteous by works and laws and that all works and labors to become righteous and be saved are in vain, as long as the nature and person are not renewed. You see now, that had he commanded to circumcise the hand or the tongue, this would have been a sign that the fault to be changed lay in the words or works; that he was favorable to the nature and person, and hated only the words and works. But now, in selecting for circumcision that part of the body which has no function except that

> nature and personal experience arise thereby,
> he gives clearly to understand that the fault
> lies in the entire estate of the nature, that its
> birth and origin are corrupt and sin.[7]

The sins I have said or done are only the symptoms. The real problem is me, myself. I am by nature sinful and unclean. With God's words in mind and a child with a life-threatening disease—well, this is the way the Old Testament Israelite would feel, I imagine, at the moment he discovers that his child in his lap has leprosy. He grasps the truth: "It must have come from me!"

A few paragraphs further along the Reformer draws a devastating conclusion from the fact that God, in the fullness of time, was born to a virgin. Luther's conclusion? We fathers are the carriers, the transmitters of sin to our sons and daughters.

> It is possible that a pure, innocent birth, nature
> and person may be derived from a woman,
> but from a man only a sinful birth, nature and
> person. Therefore circumcision was imposed
> at birth upon males only, in order to signify that
> all birth from man is sinful and condemned.[8]

The death certificate for Kyleigh Honor-Lillie Schulz lists "pulmonary edema, candida albicans sepsis, central line infection, and metabolic encephalopathy—etiology unknown" as the cause of her death. I, her father, am the mediate cause of her death. The etiology runs in a straight line from Adam to me: "Therefore, just as sin came into the world through one man, and death through sin, and so death spread to all men because all sinned" (Romans 5:12). Good Lord! Lord, have mercy.

A father. His children. Lepers all. We have to raise our voices together: "Jesus, Teacher, have mercy on us!"

We Never Learn Anything Except by Suffering

Of all that we have learned as parents, of all the lessons we think about passing on to our children, the most important are taught, not by successes in life, but by suffering.

This afternoon I am playing football with Daniel, our younger son, in the backyard. At eight years old he is full of joy and energy and questions for me. As young as I am, I cannot see him without wearing glasses. My left shoulder aches from wear and tear. My body has ears to hear the sermon of entropy and decay. It is a beneficial sermon, I suppose.

Watching Daniel ("Go out, go out! On the numbers! Great throw!"), I know that I am giving him what a father wants to give: time to play, lessons of love for play and work, for family and God. I know his

THE PROBLEM OF SUFFERING

> *mom and I have given him life. And, because of*
> *God's revelation, I know I have given him death. I*
> *cannot muster the voice to say anything more.*

Our public broadcasting station once featured a *Frontline* interview with Malcolm Muggeridge, the journalist-author who was converted to Christianity late in life. "We never learn anything except by suffering," he told William F. Buckley Jr.

Suffering is God's antidote to the pathologic optimism we fathers work so hard to maintain, that blind and bombastic optimism that boasts with William Henley, "I am the master of my fate; I am the captain of my soul." Through suffering, God teaches us that we cannot make our children happy no matter how much we give and coach and provide. Neither our children nor we are saved because of righteous things we have done. Our heads are bloodied and bowed.

Writing his study of 2 Corinthians, *Ministers of Christ*, John Meyer takes us deeply into chapter 12 (where Paul relates his suffering through that "thorn in the flesh") and calls the apostle's thorn "a powerful antitoxin, to counteract and neutralize any inclination Paul might have to be tempted to undue pride."[9]

Somewhere I heard a New Testament scholar suggest that Paul's word, which we hear translated "thorn" (it is *skolops* in Greek), could also be the technical term for "the

to render helpless

stake on which I am impaled." Suffering impales us on God's law. It bows our heads, obliges us to cast our children and ourselves on God's mercy alone.

There is an old German saying: "No cross, no crown." I used to think of that as a Christian version of the stoic "no pain, no gain" motto. But now I think of my son Stephan Paul, whenever I read about the crown and cross. One New Testament word for "crown" is *stephanos*. The first Christian martyr was Stephan. No cross, no Stephan. My son's name is a sermon on suffering. As is his entire life. No one would care for God's cross or the crown He bestows without the royal lesson of suffering. Those He loves, He chastens. We never learn anything except by suffering.

For all of my training and experience, what a terrifying realization: Am I such a slow student that this is the only way God can get through to me, through my children? More: Do they have to learn by suffering *so much*? Can't God come up with a different curriculum?

A Personal Answer

The second matter the otherwise hidden God has unveiled for us is Himself. In his journal, after his wife's suffering and death, C. S. Lewis wrote that he did not ever feel he was in danger of becoming an atheist. On the contrary, he was led to the dreadful conclusion that *this* is the kind of God He really is, the kind of God who will put a woman through years of suffering from cancer and then make her dear husband a widower.[10]

Here we come to the crux, the cross, of the entire problem of suffering. One philosopher puts it into bumper-sticker terms: If God is God, He cannot be good; if God is good, He cannot be God.

Left to our own experiences with the suffering of our children, our conclusion would be about the same as that of Harold Kushner after his son died from progeria, the rapid-aging disease. In his book *When Bad Things Happen to Good People*, he maintains, "God would like people to get what they deserve in life, but he cannot always arrange it."[11] Not true. God can always arrange things; otherwise, it isn't God we are talking about.

God is God, and God has spoken. In these last days He has spoken to us with all our questions about the suffering and dying of our sons and daughters. He has spoken to us by His Son. The crux of the matter is the cross of Calvary.

Now, I want you to understand that our children's suffering has been excruciating. Whenever you and I try to explain such things about each other's loved ones, we end up weaving their suffering together with Jesus' suffering. It is inevitable and right. *Excruciating* comes to our vocabulary from the suffering of another Son two millennia ago. It means "from the cross."

Some 2,700 years before the birth of my son and daughter, the prophet Isaiah was writing and preaching the God who would be hanged on a tree for all us sufferers. He referred to Jesus the Lord as "the Man of Sorrows, and acquainted with grief" (Isaiah 53:3). With inspired word-for-word detail, the Old Testament evangelist pointed seven centuries down the timeline to the gravity well, the nexus, of all human history.

Behold, My servant shall act wisely;
    He shall be high and lifted up, and shall be exalted.
As many were astonished at you—
    His appearance was so marred,
            beyond human semblance,
    and His form beyond that of the
            children of mankind—
so shall He sprinkle many nations;
    kings shall shut their mouths because of Him;
for that which has not been told them they see,
    and that which they have not heard
            they understand.

Who has believed what He has heard from us?
And to whom has the arm of the LORD been revealed?

For He grew up before him like a young plant,
 and like a root out of dry ground;
He had no form or majesty that we should look at Him,
 and no beauty that we should desire Him.
He was despised and rejected by men;
 a man of sorrows, and acquainted with grief;
and as one from whom men hide their faces
 He was despised, and we esteemed Him not.

Surely He has borne our griefs
 and carried our sorrows;
yet we esteemed Him stricken,
 smitten by God, and afflicted.
But He was wounded for our transgressions;
 He was crushed for our iniquities;
upon Him was the chastisement that brought us peace,
 and with His stripes we are healed.

(Isaiah 52:13–53:5)

God suffered for us and for our children! In the person of Jesus, all the fullness of the Deity suffered and died.

The *Journal of the American Medical Association* published an article by William Edwards titled "On the Physical Death of Jesus Christ."[12] While the physical cause of Jesus' death remains unclear—whether cardiorespiratory failure or cardiac rupture, Edwards rightly states that the truly important thing is not to definitively determine the cause of Jesus' death, but know that He truly *did* die.

We can talk again in medical terms about etiology, the cause of death. The cause of God's death was His Fatherly love for each of us. The punishment that brought us peace was upon Him. Not far from the Mayo Clinic (where the author of this *JAMA* article practiced), Isaiah's Lord taught me something of the Father's love.

> *Stephan, just under one year old, is being prepped for the first of many surgeries. Here at the University Hospital after patients are put under light anesthesia on the children' ward, they are bundled up and transported in red Radio Flyer wagons to surgery.*
>
> *My wife and Stephan's nurse have gone off in search of his file while I wait for the wagon. Here in the marble-floored hallway, I look down on my only son. I would do anything to spare him from what he is going through, but I cannot. For long days I have had to tell him, "No, you can't have any food or water, Sport, until after the test." I have been holding his arms and shoulders steady while nurses invade his body with intravenous needles. Stephan used most of his words to plead, "All done, Daddy? All done?" But it wasn't. It isn't.*

These minutes looking down, loving him and wondering, I think back to a sermon study I'd been doing at his bedside last night. A text from an epistle by John, the disciple who wrote, "God so loved the world, that He gave His only Son" (John 3:16). How can a Father stand by—no, actively continue to act this way with His Son?

A few weeks later I am preaching a Lenten sermon to my congregation. From the pulpit I say, "As much as I love you, never, never would I give up my son for you. But God gave His for us." What I do not mention is that in my study, crafting the sermon, I could only ask aghast, over and over, "How could You?" Yet such are the thoughts of the Father for His Son. And for us sons.

Still, here we are at the gravesides and the bedsides of our suffering sons and daughters. We are "children [of God], then heirs—heirs of God and fellow heirs with Christ, provided we suffer with Him in order that we may also be glorified with Him" (Romans 8:17). The Scriptures are clear, but our children and we go on suffering.

Fear and Trembling

In the midst of suffering, God administers His test. It is a test in the most heart-wrenching format of all. "God loves you: True or False?" It is our faith being dislocated, joint from socket, on God's rack. It is the test of contradiction.

Contradiction. It makes our cross even heavier. Or is it that the apparent contradiction makes us weaker under the heavy load? We know God's ability, and we know His promise. In the here and now we raise our eyes in horror from the bed where our child is pierced with IV lines and wounded from surgery after surgery. We read our Bibles and we watch our children. We cry out (or cry in), "Lord, I believe, but . . . *how can You keep doing this?*"

The New Testament translator J. B. Phillips wrote a book with the title *Your God Is Too Small*. For those of us who say, "Call me Job," the problem with suffering is that our God is too big. During suffering, God seems to be too imminent, much too close. In the middle of his test, Job begged the Lord,

I loathe my life; I would not live forever.
　　Leave me alone, for my days are a breath.
What is man, that You make so much of him,
　　and that You set your heart on him,
visit him every morning
　　and test him every moment?
How long will You not look away from me,
　　nor leave me alone till I swallow my spit?
If I sin, what do I do to You,
　　　　You watcher of mankind?

Why have You made me Your mark?
Why have I become a burden to You?
Why do You not pardon my transgression
and take away my iniquity?
For now I shall lie in the earth;
You will seek me, but I shall not be. (Job 7:16–21)

Once, for a Philosophy of God course, I had asked my class, "In your experience, does the problem of evil and suffering make people doubt God's existence or His essence?" One of the students shared her concern for a friend: "It's not that she doesn't believe in God. She even believes that everything in the Bible is true. She just doesn't believe that what God says is true *for her.*" There it is.

In the working out of all things for our good, God's actions toward us leave us with exactly that question: "*Credo,* I believe. But look what You are doing! Look at what You are doing to my child. Aren't Your promises good for me and mine?"

We are back to the believer's question: Why? But, I must tell you, it is not a question asked quietly or thoughtfully or reverently. It is a question wrung out of a bleeding soul who is being pressed ever tighter in God's vise. In the day of trouble, we do not "call upon God" stoically and with good grace; we scream and beg and plead and despair.

Years ago, when he was only four, Stephan fell into a coma.

Saturdays at Children's Hospital are true Sabbaths. Today there will be no surgeries or tests. Only a few visits from doctors or medical students. Right after the first blood draw of the day at 6 a.m. we decide to watch cartoons. We are laughing and chatting about going home early the next week. I have in my hands a list of food for home cooking, that Stephan, with a great deal of relish, has just finished dictating.

Abruptly, Stephan starts talking nonsense. "My toothbrush," he shouts. "Get my toothbrush! My nose, my head. It's in my head!" he screams. Incoherent. He kicks at me. Buzz the nurse. A quick page to the doctor on call. Too slow, too slow. Violent squirming. Restraints. More shouting.

Without warning, Stephan is limp and very, very quiet.

A nurse clears the way as I rush, son in arms, down two flights of stairs to meet the doctor at the CAT scanner. Stephan? Stephan! I felt God ripping him from my arms.

They need to peer into his head to look for—for what? The protective vest is heavy as I stand guard next to the scanner, as I stand at the angel's post. Beside my boy. Comatose.

Two days and two nights pass in the pediatric intensive care unit. Not a word, not a flicker of an eyelid. The flight-for-life helicopter flies overhead. Twice. I wonder if his soul will be the next to take flight. (Stephan always wanted to be a pilot. . . .)

Will we ever play chess again, watch a ballgame on TV, and laugh at our favorite handful of jokes? "Lord!" I find myself praying in disbelief, "Not my little boy! What about Your other miracles— children with epilepsy and demon-possessed? You cured them! What about Stephan? Please! Please! Please!"

It is the Abraham test. As Luther says in his Genesis lectures:

Abraham was actually tempted by God Him- self, not concerning a woman, gold, silver, death, or life but concerning a contradiction of Holy Scripture. Here God is clearly contradict- ing Himself; for how do these statements agree: "Through Isaac shall your descendants be named" (Gen. 21:12) and "Take your son, and sacrifice him"? . . . God, who formerly seemed to be his best friend, now appears to have become an enemy and a tyrant.[13]

Søren Kierkegaard says that we must approach this story with "fear and trembling." He points out, "There were countless generations which knew by rote, word for word, the story of Abraham—how many were made sleepless by it?"[14] Many of us, including Magdalena Luther's father, have agonized long days and nights at the contradiction between God's promise to love us as our dear Father and His abusive actions toward us and our children.

Parents are filled with fear and trembling in these sleepless nights of giving medication every two hours and answering constant apnea alarms. Having the resident doctor ask as your child struggles to draw breath after respiratory arrest, "Should we put her on a respirator or not? It's your choice"—now there is a time to wonder if our God has now become our enemy.

There is no hiding place in the valley of suffering . . . *except in God Himself*.

The answer to the test is to persevere and to study up on the upcoming chapters of the story. Think of Psalm 73. Asaph opens with our usual confession of God's goodness. "Truly God is good to Israel" (Psalm 73:1). But then he tells God how his feet had almost slipped fatally as he saw that the unbelievers were healthy and wealthy while "all the day long I have been stricken and rebuked every morning" (Psalm 73:14). Only fear of further harming the children holds him back. "If I had said, 'I will speak thus,' I would have betrayed the generation of your children" (Psalm 73:15). The only thing left to do is to fix our eyes on Jesus and to look heavenward.

> Whom have I in heaven but You?
>   And there is nothing on earth that
>   I desire besides You.
> My flesh and my heart may fail,
>   but God is the strength of my heart
>   and my portion forever. (Psalm 73:25–26)

The facts of heaven and the resurrection of the body comprise Abraham's answer to God's test. "[Abraham] considered that God was able even to raise [Isaac] from the dead, from which, figuratively speaking, he did receive him back" (Hebrews 11:19). Lewis tells us in *The Problem of Pain* that our main failure in this matter of evil and suffering has been that we just do not to talk about heaven as the counterbalance to suffering. In fact, he thinks we Christians are inexplicably shy about even mentioning heaven.[15]

I shall not be shy about discussing heaven. An upcoming chapter is about that never-ending story. But for a moment, here in the middle of this dreadful test from God, the pass or fail question is "How do I know that Jesus has a place for me and mine in heaven?" It seems all too clear that He doesn't love us. God looks like an abusive father. Notwithstanding, the Bible insists that this is appearance versus reality, in the final analysis. Still, the appearance is our here-and-now reality. The ultimate reality is beyond what our eyes see or our minds can conceive.

Reality left its permanent mark on my heart when I was a high school teacher. During summer vacation, one of my students was killed in a tragic accident. Biking to his summer job, Matt was struck and killed by a truck that inexplicably veered into him. For his funeral sermon, I brought Psalm 31:15 to his grieving family and friends: "My times are in Your hand."

I am sure that Matt was taken to Abraham's side that day. How do I know? As part of an end-of-year quiz, I had asked Matt and his sophomore classmates, "How do you know that Jesus died and rose for you?" Matt had written his answer: "God so loved the world that He gave His one and only Son." He had underlined "world" three times and penciled in "That's how!"

I cannot justify God's ways with my children. Job spoke for all parents when he wrote four thousand years ago, "Behold, He snatches away; who can turn him back? Who will say to Him, 'What are You doing?' " It was Job's children, all ten killed in one day, that God snatched away. Like Job, I am asking, "What are you doing?" (Job 9:12). I do not wish to anger the Lord, but, since He first invited us to call upon Him, I am asking what can justify His actions.

He gave Stephan back to us after his coma; He took Kyleigh from us after her excruciating illness.

But one fact remains true despite their suffering and my agony, namely, God has justified us. He has declared us sinners "Not guilty!" He has given us divine approval and His own Fatherly love in His Son. Paul proclaims what we Lutheran believers know as "universal justification." This is the one and only reason we can persevere in the face of such suffering. In his epistle to the Romans (the same epistle in which he tells us that our present sufferings cannot compare with the glory to be unveiled in us [Romans 8:18]), Paul writes it out, plain and simple:

> For there is no distinction: for all have sinned and fall short of the glory of God, and are justified by His grace as a gift, through the redemption that is in Christ Jesus, whom God put forward as a propitiation by His blood, to be received by faith. This was to show God's righteousness, because in His divine forbearance He had passed over former sins.
> (Romans 3:22–25)

We may want theodicy, to justify the ways of God to man, but God's will is for us to suffer so that He may teach us the mystery of His love—not by justifying His ways, but by justifying us. We think that we need answers, but God knows that we need Jesus Himself. The British pastor-poet George Herbert touches on this interchange in "The Agony":

> Philosophers have measured mountains,
> Fathomed the depths of seas, of states,
>> and kings,
> Walked with a staff to heav'n,
>> and tracèd fountains:
> But there are two vast, spacious things,
> The which to measure it doth more
> behove;
> Yet few there are that sound them,
>> Sin and Love.
>
> Who would know Sin, let him repair
> Unto Mount Olivet; there shall he see
> A Man so wrung with pains,
>> that all his hair,
> His skin, his garments bloody be.
> Sin is that press and vice,
>> which forceth pain

> To hunt his cruel food through ev'ry vein.
> Who knows not Love, let him assay
> And taste that juice which on the
>   cross a pike
> Did set again abroach; then let him say
> If ever he did taste the like.
> Love is that liquor, sweet and most divine,
> Which my God feels as blood,
>   but I as wine.[16]

I have tasted God's love. I would like to tell you that it is always a rich, delicious feast, but often, watching my children suffering, I have to be satisfied with a tincture, just a taste. For the time being.

Like a patient just waking up from surgery, I feel groggy. Pain. Hunger, yes. Some nausea. I am thirsty but leery of drinking too deep too fast. In and out, I am uncertain. At this point in my life, I cannot jump up and leap for joy. The sites of the Surgeon's amputations still throb. He will have to watch my wounds for infection, I think, very closely indeed.

CHAPTER 3

Baptized to Die

He who is baptized is condemned to die. . . .
"We were buried with Christ by baptism into death."
The sooner a person dies after baptism, the sooner
is his baptism completed.

—Martin Luther,
"The Holy and Blessed Sacrament of Baptism"[1]

The sterile water was not sterile after all. Let me take you back nearly one year before my daughter's death, to her rebirth day.

> *Warm air, distant baby sounds. This is the natal nursery of our community hospital. Kyleigh is experiencing episodes of apnea when she simply stops breathing and turns a dusky color. An ambulance and transport team are on the way to transport this two-day-old to the city's level three neonatal nursery. "They are the best," a friend had said before her birth. "If anything goes wrong, that's the place for her to be." It is time to give up my fourth child for adoption.*

THE PROBLEM OF SUFFERING

Speak the ancient God-given words: "I baptize you in the name of the Father." Three fingers dip into a baby food jar labeled "sterile water" and I rub wet fingers across the dusky forehead. "And of the Son." More sterile water, water on my fingers, on a dusky forehead and on my face. A whisper: "And in the name of the Holy Ghost." A third trickle, from one generation to the next.

It is finished. The pastor's voice cracks as he speaks the blessing, the father makes the sign of the cross over head and heart. Spoken sotto voce, under the a vague whisper *breath: "The Lord watch over thy going out (out into the ambulance) and thy coming in (how far from heaven is she, Lord?) from this day forth and even forevermore." The sign of the cross. The sign of His gallows.*

The water is not sterile. It is not plain water, but water used by God's command and connected with God's Word.

It is burial water. We baptize our children in order to bury them.

Do you not know that all of us who have been baptized into Christ Jesus were baptized into His death? We were buried therefore with Him by baptism into death, in order that, just as Christ was raised from the dead by the glory of the Father, we too might walk in newness of life. (Romans 6:3–4)

It is resurrection water. We baptize our children as the means of transplanting them into Jesus' own rising from death.

> For if we have been united with Him in a death like His, we shall certainly be united with Him in a resurrection like His. (Romans 6:5)

It is the water of life through death.

> Now if we have died with Christ, we believe that we will also live with Him. We know that Christ, being raised from the dead, will never die again; death no longer has dominion over Him. (Romans 6:8–9)

As we hurry to follow the ambulance to the next hospital, I remember fleetingly Luther's reminder in "The Holy and Blessed Sacrament of Baptism." He speaks of Baptism as being completed after the Last Day. But all I can think of is his statement, "The sooner a person dies after baptism, the sooner is his baptism completed."

It was too much for Him to ask of Abraham. It is certainly too much for Him to ask of me. "Go warn the children of God of the terrible speed of mercy." That's what Flannery O'Connor's character Bishop from *The Violent*

Bear It Away knows in his blood. "Once it's done, it's done forever." I have drowned my little girl to save her.

The Medicines of God's Mercy

So we mourn. We believers, "we Cross-tians," we might as well say, we mourn with hope in the middle of suffering. Hope is what the God of all mercy gives us through the Word and Absolution, Baptism, and the Lord's Supper. These are the ways and means of God's mercy to us. Through them, hope becomes our method.

Stephan took medications twice daily. His meds were an obvious blessing to his health. For Kyleigh, we tried an uncountable series of different formulas. She relied on more than a dozen medications, at first delivered through her G-tube; later, they were transmitted intravenously. Sometimes our best medications are an effective therapy to prolong life; sometimes our best medicines are simply ineffective.

About effective prescriptions. In confirmation and Bible classes I use the diagram of a large reservoir connected to a pipeline with three faucets. The water is God's grace, the gift of forgiveness itself won by Jesus with His life and death and resurrection. God the Holy Ghost applies this grace-gift to us personally and effectively through the three faucets, if you will, of Baptism, the Lord's Supper, and the

Word (including Absolution), the same grace-alone gift coming through each of the three faucets. I'm thinking of replacing that reservoir and pipeline with an intravenous bag, tube, and syringe.

Call them "the medicines of mercy." These medications of grace are always effective, even when—especially when—the patient dies. In one passage of that medicinal Word, Paul writes to us of Jesus' second coming "from heaven with a cry of command, with the voice of an archangel, and with the sound of the trumpet of God. And the dead in Christ will rise first. Then we who are alive, who are left, will be caught up together with them in the clouds to meet the Lord in the air, and so we will always be with the Lord." Then the apostolic injunction: "Therefore encourage one another with these words" (1 Thessalonians 4:16–17, 18).

Refusing to Be Comforted

Yet, have you seen what I've seen? God's words of comfort are not always comforting to us. Our grieving in the blitz of God's severe mercy is indeed substantial. Notwithstanding our discomfort, He has promised to bring His mercy to us only through these medicines of grace.

There are times, then, when we sufferers feel no comfort whatsoever in His Word. Perhaps you, too, have read C. S. Lewis's *A Grief Observed*, the basis for the play and two movies called *Shadowlands*. It is Lewis's personal journal, which he kept after his bride, Joy, died from cancer. She (and he with her) had suffered for four years. And then she died.

In one paragraph, the widowed professor tells us how he felt when a friend spoke to him of the Thessalonians passage we read a moment ago, namely, that the comfort of Scripture is apparently meant for better believers than we are.[2] Kyleigh gained everything when Jesus took her to be with Him, but my wife and I will never get to read to her again or teach her to ride a bike. I will never walk her down the aisle for her wedding or baptize the grandchildren that she and her husband would have given us.

We will be talking about Kyleigh's never-ending gain, but for the present, we consider the loss to those of us left behind. There is, inevitably, an aspect of "refusing to be comforted," because she is gone.

Let me tell you what you can expect to run into if God brings great suffering into your life. Expect an "explanatory space," a barrier around us suffering and grieving people where talk about God's incarnation and presence and love seem irrelevant. These articles of faith are relevant, of course. Very relevant. But they seem useless. Looking down on your daughter's coffin, everything seems useless. And for far longer than you may imagine.

Isn't this what we see in the real-life stories of God's people? At the start of Job's story, Eliphaz, Bildad, and Zophar recognized and respected this force field around their bereaved and stricken friend.

> And when they saw him from a distance, they did not recognize him. And they raised their voices and wept, and they tore their robes and sprinkled dust on their heads toward heaven. And they sat with him on the ground seven days and seven nights, and no one spoke a word to him, for they saw that his suffering was very great. (Job 2:12–13)

Paul recognizes and respects this as well. He urges us to "let love be genuine" and tells us to "weep with those who weep" (Romans 12:9, 15).

There is a special need for us to mourn with those who are mourning for the death of a child. Donald Deffner speaks compassionately about this in *At the Death of a Child*: "Your grieving and mourning is a normal and necessary process to work through. And it may take longer than you or your dearest friends may realize."[3]

I love you, Kyleigh! I miss you, and that is why I mourn. I love you, Stephan, my son. In you, my sons and my daughters, I am blessed. You are why I hope. You are why I mourn. For a long while. For the rest of my life on earth.

Under the Mercy

When Sheldon Vanauken wrote about the death of his wife and sweetheart, Jean, he titled his book of conversion and Christian joy *A Severe Mercy*. He spoke about being there with Jean as she blindly reached for his face and then died, how he looked forward to his own death and the first thing that he would do upon reaching heaven. He expected to find Jean's hand and listen to her voice again. His mourning and his hoping he categorized as being "under the mercy."[4]

My grief as a father is different from Vanauken's grief as a husband. I think of many couples I have served whose children have been stillborn. They have no memories to cherish of shared times with their infants. Our Kyleigh was incapable of reaching out to find the faces of her mother or father. She did not yet have a voice for anything other than crying out in pain.

So we grieving parents, most of all, must live "under the mercy," trusting exclusively in God that we can be fathers and mothers to our children in His heaven. Only He can fortify our souls for these long years of such mourning and hoping. Only He can do this, through His medicines of mercy.

Only God can give us the view of heaven's reality behind and beyond our present suffering. We need intensive and critical care from Word and Sacraments in His church.

In my church's hymnal is a responsive prayer the minister prays just prior to Holy Communion, "Through these means of grace, you send the Holy Spirit into our hearts and unite us to Jesus and to the whole Christian Church on earth."[5] In reality, Jesus' sacrament joins us (in fact, not in mere symbol) with the whole Christian Church on earth and in heaven. The church militant and the church triumphant are both at the Communion rail. No semi-sacrament; no semi-communion. It's the complete circle of all of us in Christ at the Eucharist.

Let me make an important distinction about the sacraments. It is often assumed that the sacraments are generic and objective, but that is not so. Our grief is for a specific person, as is mine for my daughter Kyleigh, *and so are the sacraments*. They are not internal achievements but external realities that teach us to cling to God's external and particular work *pro nobis*, as Luther emphasized, for us and for our children. Sacraments such as Baptism are Christ's means for rescuing us from our doubts and insecurities, even from our insecurities of faith, and putting us into communion with Him personally.[6]

And now, before returning graveside, I would like to talk with you about that complete circle. God's Bible is not a workbook on the stages of grieving. It is the story of the God who is real. This is the real-life story of our lives *together*, with them in Him, even after our children suffer and die.

65

The Never-Ending Story

I fear to weep for thee,
Because I am so instructed
That the Son of the Kingdom hath removed thee
To His bright habitation.

— St. Ephraim Syrus, "On the Death of a Child"

While serving my first congregation in South Dakota where Stephan was born, I came to know the work of Harvey Dunn. A collection of his paintings had come to Aberdeen.

"The Son of the Middle Border" is what the exhibit curator calls him. She is glad to talk; as my wife, Paula, and I look closely at one painting, the curator tells us its story.

A typical Great Plains sky dominates: a suspension of dust and dusty clouds brooding overhead, becoming sky blue and cloud white only at the horizon. The view to that far, faraway horizon is unimpeded. Bottom middle: a cluster of darker brown shapes against the dark brown waves of the prairie. The dark shapes occupy a small enclosure of rough wooden posts and barbed wire fence. Outside the fence, a buggy and two empty buckboards, their horses grazing toward the enclosure. Inside, fewer than a dozen souls. The men's hats are in hand; heads bowed. Only one head is lifted. The preacher is reading. To his left, a man has his head and back bent as if he would fall onto a heap of earth. A blue-dressed woman stands to his left, also bent, but with her arm across the shoulder of a young child standing close, close. There they stand, under the great dust-colored plains sky.

It is a burial.

The curator is explaining. "Not long ago out here on the plains, when a child died, it would be up to the father to build the coffin, usually that same day. And the children often died, you know."

We have a copy of his piece in our home. The title of Dunn's painting? "I Am the Resurrection and the Life."

The Weight of Glory

I did not build my daughter's coffin. But if I had, I would have made it heavier.

One April afternoon, three days short of Kyleigh's first birthday, I was carrying her casket. I had no eye for the sky or the horizon, just for my wife and four children, one past all suffering, as I took the all-too-small white casket and gently laid her down next to her grave.

"May God the Father who created this body, may God the Son who redeemed this body together with its soul, may God the Holy Ghost who sanctified this body, keep it safe until the resurrection of all flesh."

Words give weight to our lives, to our suffering. In our Lutheran Confessions, we maintain that we cannot apprehend God *nisi per Verbum*, except through the Word. In the first place, this means that Jesus Christ is the exclusive Way to God (John 14:6) and God's final word to all people (Hebrews 1:1–3). Second, it means that, in the words of the Bible, God gives us the words to approach Him with our grief. The hope and confidence is that, since He spoke first, we are invited and expected to respond to Him. God's words give weight, heaviness, to the suffering, death, and lives of our children.

Such weight God's Word gives! It is the weight of glory, the glory of God's one and only Son credited to each of us sinners. Our children are weighty and important, not because of the things they've accomplished—our Kyleigh never had the opportunity to live her life for her Lord—not because they live on in our memories, but because God has made them so. Twice-made: by creation and by redemption. By water and blood, by Jesus' Baptism and Jesus' death, applied to them personally by God the Holy Spirit. In suffering, in death, in life, our children are in reality forever glorious.

The Way Home

The suffering and dying of our children, we are led to believe, is not the end of the story. It is, God tells us, only a comparatively brief preface.

Sooner or later, we all come home. We came home from the cemetery after our daughter and sister's burial. I came home after my December mourning, though I left my Christmas wreath. Home to my grieving wife. Home to my surviving children. Already wearied from a decade of hospitalizations and emergencies with Stephan, we were exhausted beyond description from Kyleigh's agony and death. Nearly two years after Kyleigh's funeral and with Stephan feeling the best he ever has, we were coming to feel more at home in God's story.

Have you seen the movie *The Neverending Story*? It's based on a book with the same name by Michael Ende.

Atreyu, the boy warrior; Falkor, the luck-dragon; the Rock Biter; castles; and good and evil populate the land of Fantasia. "Once upon a time a little boy named Bastian opened a special book and was transported into a magical land of danger and enchantment." Bastian entered physically into the never-ending story through a book.

We are taken into the Great Story through the Book of books. This is why God saw to it that John, Moses, and all the holy men of God wrote down these sixty-six books of His words: "These are written so that you may believe that Jesus is the Christ, the Son of God, and that by believing you may have life in His name" (John 20:31).

Stephan and I loved to read together. The longer the days and nights would get, the more we loved to read—especially science fiction and fantasy stories. Our stories became not only shared time, but welcome escape—other realities to visit, to enjoy, to look forward to. Stories of elvish lords and sturdy hobbits led us to speak of guardian angels ("Kyleigh can see them all the time, can't she, Dad?") and faithful saints ("Steph, I think you are the real Frodo; just look at your scars!") For us, it is not the willing suspension of disbelief; it is the eager practice of what we have learned from the Scriptures. "Now faith is the assurance of things hoped for, the conviction of things not seen" (Hebrews 11:1).

Following James' point that every good gift is from the

same God, let me introduce you to a few favorite stories that give us glimpses of heaven.

Paula and I regularly read children's stories with Kara, Stephan, Daniel, and Kyleigh. One is Kenneth Grahame's *The Wind in the Willows*. Some years ago a friend, who knew chronic suffering in her life, gave it to us as a gift. During our Christmas hospitalization with Kyleigh in California, we followed the friends in their adventures along The River: gentle Mole and adventurous Ratty, wise old Badger and Mr. Toad. *The Wind* was one of the books I read to Kyleigh (twice) her last week with us.

We have long enjoyed C. S. Lewis's *The Chronicles of Narnia* and George MacDonald's stories of princesses, goblins, and the North Wind.

One series in particular is a favorite. Stephan and I have a special love for *The Hobbit* and *The Lord of the Rings* trilogy by J. R. R. Tolkien. I cannot tell you how many months of nights we have followed the quests of Bilbo and Frodo, the short, stout, steadfast, and hairy-toed hobbits of Middle-Earth. I still have our well-worn copy of Karen Wynn Fonstad's *The Atlas of Middle-Earth*, 210 pages of indexes, road maps, fortresses, and diagrams that show the way from the Shire to Mount Doom.

There is a last map in our atlas with the caption "The Road Home." It features an unmistakable arrow pointing westward, across the sea, away from the hobbit's dear and familiar home country. The arrow is labeled "The Straight Way." The Tolkien epic closes with Gandalf (a good, wise wizard) welcoming Frodo (the intrepid hobbit) on board a ship.

Three worthy heroes, Frodo's comrades, Merry and Pippin, as well as his dear friend, Samwise, must stay behind for awhile yet. Perhaps you already know the closing scene in which three of the four steadfast friends have to bid goodbye to Frodo. Frodo, weary and wounded, exhausted from fighting the good fight, sails away to the West. The three friends must return home without him.

> "Yes," said Gandalf; "for it will be better to ride back three together than one alone. Well, here at last, dear friends, on the shores of the Sea comes the end of our fellowship in Middle-earth. Go in peace! I will not say: do not weep; for not all tears are an evil."[1]

For us survivors left behind, the evening deepens to darkness, doesn't it? But sometimes we are given glimpses of the real Haven.

Stephan once said, "The West is really a place, isn't it, Dad?" Yes, oh, yes. One of your sisters is already there. You and Mom and Daniel and Kara and I will be going there soon. At Kyleigh's grave we would stand together and know together that not all tears are an evil. We always face the West.

Tolkien was a Christian writer. He was, in fact, instrumental in C. S. Lewis's conversion to Christianity. In Tolkien's essay "On Fairy-Stories," he grants that we read fantasy for escape from our world of suffering. The sub-creator of Middle Earth argues that such escape is very healthy for us sufferers. A person who has been imprisoned tries to escape. If he cannot escape, he thinks and talks a great deal about the world, the *real* world, outside his cell. He has to live by faith, not by sight, so he spends a great deal of time with stories and discussions of the larger world that is, for the time being, invisible to him.[2]

The Christian story, the Bible, is not escapist; rather, it is revelation, God's words to us. Consider what is real and what is fantasy. Let me tell you a real-life story of The Way Home.

It is early on a Wednesday morning in April. Both Paula and I have been spending the night with Kyleigh in her room at Children's Hospital. A hand on my shoulder, Rachel weeping for her children in my wife's voice. "Wake up, wake up. She's going." Kyleigh's labored breath has become less of a labor. The electronic monitor tells its story. Her heart rate is slipping from 212 beats a minute into the 190s and even the 180s. Kyleigh's brave little heart keeps slowing. One hour. Two.

We minister to her, talking quietly to her, and take turns holding our little girl. Knowing that she can't see, but believing all along that she can hear, we feel it important to keep talking and reassuring her. I sing "I am Jesus' Little Lamb" for her a last time and then once more. Quietly, quietly. Don't jar her fragile system into a seizure. Please, oh please.

Running my fingers through her baby-fine brown hair. Gently, gently. I lean a bit more toward her head as we sit in the rocking chair (carefully, carefully) to say, "It's all right, Princess. You can go. We want you here but I know it's too, too hard. Be happy. And save me a place." I see her open her right eye just a slit and look up at me. Impossible, I know; she is blind. But not for long.

Back in her mother's lap. Heart rate 120. Near normal, because she is dying. Inside, I pray for a miraculous cure and think, "What a proof of Your glory it will be. This sick, handicapped child miraculously well!" And then I take back the petition. It is a cruel, selfish thing for a father to ask.

The monitor respectfully reports a heartbeat waning to zero. Nothing can be done. Her mother's arms hold her, her father's hand is on her warm, curly-haired head—but she is gone. Good-bye, Kyleigh. God be with you. Be . . . with . . . God!

Gone. Gone! As I think about this dreadful night, my mind goes back a few months to a pericope that I never wanted to preach during the Christmas and Epiphany season, though I did.

At the slaughter of the boys in Bethlehem by Herod's order, the apostle writes,

> A voice was heard in Ramah,
>   weeping and loud lamentation,
> Rachel weeping for her children;
>   she refused to be comforted,
>   because they are no more.
>
> (Matthew 2:18)

This is Jeremiah and Matthew's language for our grief. Call me Rachel. Every suffering believer may claim Job's name, but we who have lost our children must take a second name as well.

"Because they are no more." No, the apostle is not saying that those anguished mothers did not have the advanced understanding of heaven that we moderns do. They knew the story of Enoch. They knew their Wisdom Literature. They knew Job 19 and Ecclesiastes 12. It's just that this is the way it looks and feels, whether in Bethlehem or in our own homes. Kyleigh is gone. I can't find her anywhere!

Why these tears? Why do we cry at the story of friends setting sail for the West or at the thought of a child being gone, that is, being somewhere else? It's because we have a sense of *fore-nostalgia*, the hope that God has engraved in our being through those means of grace, the hope in the wider, currently invisible reality. In this hope, we lift up our eyes even now, before the trumpet of God sounds, scouring the horizon for the Eden to come, on tiptoe.

The cry of "No" is very much in place here, in this world where our children suffer and die. But we have God's words, words from outside the walls, breathed into His writers once imprisoned here with us. And God's words teach us that these winsome stories of Narnia and Middle Earth and the back of the North Wind are shimmering reflections of deep reality.

It is the Truth Himself who once explained, "I am the resurrection and the life. Whoever believes in Me, though he die, yet shall he live" (John 11:25). He is still telling the story. Paul wrote to his friends, "You yourselves are our letter of recommendation, written on our hearts, to be known and read by all" (2 Corinthians 3:2). Our children are being written into God's story.

Our Shadow Box

We have a shadow box that was, for many years, on the hallway wall just outside the bedroom where Kyleigh slept when she could be at home with us. Behind its glass door, you can see her Baptism certificate and several dried roses from her funeral. There is a pair of her little shoes and her copy of a touchable book, *Pat the Bunny*. The box includes a picture of her brothers and sister, which had been taped to her Isolette while she was in the neonatal ICU. And there is a small, rose-framed picture of Kyleigh. But she does not exist there herself. Nor does she live on in our memories. The pictures and memories are artifacts; they are not my living child.

You may have seen the play or one of the movies titled *Shadowlands*. The title is drawn from Lewis's *The Last Battle*, an allegorical tale about the end of time in the land of Narnia. In the story the untamed lion, Aslan (that is, Jesus), is talking with the children at the center of the story after their sudden death. In the story, Aslan explains to the children that they have just died in a train wreck. This means, the Savior says, that school is over and vacation has begun. They have, in fact, just now awakened from sleep and are at last truly awake. It's morning![3]

Please don't mistake Lewis's analogy. Heaven is not the dreamworld, something too good to be true, a shadow of our imagination. Heaven is real. This life, this great tribulation, is the Shadowland. Kyleigh's shadow box is in the Shadowlands. As are we. This, too, will pass away.

Further Up and Further In

After Kyleigh's death, many well-meaning friends sent cards and notes saying, "How you loved her! As long as you keep loving her, she will live on in your heart and memory."

We do not want our children to live in the virtual reality of our memories, avatars of themselves. We want them to have life and have it to the fullest! We want them to be genuinely and unendingly happy. We want them to be in heaven. We want God's will to be done. And it is. With or without our wanting what is best, for that matter.

In the suffering of our children, God reviews with us the reality of hell so that we change our thinking and actually pray—not simply for their health and immediate happiness—but that He will take them to heaven, to live with Him there.

"The greatest is the pain of loss." When our son, Stephan, was just four years old, quite sick and without a working diagnosis, we had to make a run into the hospital's emergency room. Along with everything else, Stephan had developed bruises on both his legs. Right at the top of his socks, he had angry purple ridges all around his right and left ankles.

The physician in the ER cannot follow my description of Stephan's long-term symptoms. Nor can she figure out the cause of those bruises. What kind of doctor is this?! She asks to see me on the other side of the examining room curtain and tells me she has no choice but to report this as a case of suspected child abuse. Stephan and I will not be allowed to go home.

Much later. We have been told to wait in this small windowless room while a social worker is summoned to interview him and determine if I have abused and bruised my child. For three hours we sit. Stephan is hungry and already worn out from two hours of waiting in the ER. I consider the real likelihood that someone may, in a few hours, separate us just when he needs me most! At the same time, I must be cheerful and good-humored for his sake. Knowing that I have not bruised him, I realize that someone may discover, plain as day after the fact, something else I should have done long ago to get my son's condition diagnosed and treated before it came to this.

(Only much later would a different physician discover that Stephan's small blood vessels had become fragile from his liver condition, that his ankles had been bruised by the elastic on his socks and sweatpants.) But in this purgatorial room I

can't help imagining the pain of separation and loss. Emily Dickinson writes, "Parting is all we know of heaven / And all we need of hell." A hint of hell. All a father needs.

On Stephan's first Christmas, Paula and I had to give him frequent aerosol treatments. That holiday, his doctors were beginning to suggest that he had cystic fibrosis. With the mask over his nose and mouth, we would sing Christmas carols while the mist machine hissed.

So, against the pain of forever-loss we kept singing the ancient cradle songs and carols to our son. The last stanza of "Away in a Manger" was especially touching. To be reminded how close heaven is and how soon God might answer our prayer to "Bless all the dear children in Thy tender care / And take us to heaven to live with Thee there" always brought tears (sometimes defiant, sometimes grateful) into my eyes. It still does.

After These Things

God wants us to live right now in the certainty that heaven is not far away from us. Nor are our loved ones. In the mid-90s of the first century AD God opened a door to bring the apostle John from the island of Patmos into heaven, to see the reality of our family home. Then, back to Patmos to write some of it down. In Revelation 7, John reports,

After this I looked, and behold, a great multitude that no one could number, from every nation, from all tribes and peoples and languages, standing before the throne and before the Lamb, clothed in white robes, with palm branches in their hands, and crying out with a loud voice, "Salvation belongs to our God who sits on the throne, and to the Lamb!" And all the angels were standing around the throne and around the elders and the four living creatures, and they fell on their faces before the throne and worshiped God, saying, "Amen! Blessing and glory and wisdom and thanksgiving and honor and power and might be to our God forever and ever! Amen."

Then one of the elders addressed me, saying, "Who are these, clothed in white robes, and from where have they come?" I said to him, "Sir, you know." And he said to me, "These are the ones coming out of the great tribulation. They have washed their robes and made them white in the blood of the Lamb.

"Therefore they are before the throne of God,
and serve Him day and night in His temple;
and He who sits on the throne will shelter
them with His presence.

"They shall hunger no more, neither thirst anymore;
the sun shall not strike them,
nor any scorching heat.

"For the Lamb in the midst of the throne
will be their shepherd,
and He will guide them to springs of living water,
and God will wipe away every tear
from their eyes." (Revelation 7:9–17)

That Wednesday morning, though Kyleigh "was no more" to our perception, she was—she *is*, she *exists*, she *lives* right now—in the inner circle of heaven within constant sight of her Jesus. Eyes that were clouded with keratin scales that morning are now bright with the sight of glory: His and hers. Hands that could not be coached by any amount of care and therapy to grasp my fingers are waving branches to celebrate her King. Lips that before could only form her cries are practicing a new song this very minute. Our little girl is in chorus with Miriam and Mary:

"My strength and my defense is the Lord who has saved me! My soul magnifies the Lord, and my spirit rejoices in God my Savior! We are saved by our God, who sits on the throne and by the Lamb!"

Standing at her grave (it's her body, not Kyleigh, that sleeps until Redemption Day), I know that heaven and she are close at hand. Really. Our here and now is Flatland; heaven is the more real, more substantial, more concrete dimension on which we depend. I look for the resurrection of the body and life everlasting.

This is the view from heaven with which C. S. Lewis closes the Chronicles of Narnia, where he speaks of life in heaven as the authentic "happily ever after" wished for in our traditional children's stories. What Aslan went on to tell the children and what began to happen were, Lewis writes, "so great and wonderful that I cannot write them down." The children who had died were just beginning the first chapter of a Great Story that is unending and in which "every chapter is better than the one before."[4]

A Deeper Communion

In his Narnia books, Lewis urged the children to keep going "further up and further in" to heaven itself. T. S. Eliot puts it this way in his *Four Quartets*:

We must be still and still moving
 Into another intensity
For a further union, a deeper communion.[5]

What Eliot does not express and what modern and twenty-first century writers on heaven generally neglect is the truth that heaven is not Newtonian space, a region that is filled, more or less, with saints and angels and manifestations of God's glory. Heaven is Einsteinian. Whereas we know from physics that space and time are relative to each other, so that we cannot talk about space on the one hand and time on the other, but must think about space-time, we know from the Bible that heaven is relative to our Lord, so that we cannot talk about heaven without Jesus, but must think about heaven-with-Jesus. Think of Revelation and the "physics" of John's first chapter.

> I, John, your brother and partner in the tribulation and the kingdom and the patient endurance that are in Jesus, was on the island called Patmos on account of the word of God and the testimony of Jesus. I was in the Spirit on the Lord's day, and I heard behind me a loud voice like a trumpet saying, "Write what

you see in a book and send it to the seven churches, to Ephesus and to Smyrna and to Pergamum and to Thyatira and to Sardis and to Philadelphia and to Laodicea."

Then I turned to see the voice that was speaking to me, and on turning I saw seven golden lampstands, and in the midst of the lampstands one like a son of man, clothed with a long robe and with a golden sash around his chest. The hairs of his head were white, like white wool, like snow. His eyes were like a flame of fire, his feet were like burnished bronze, refined in a furnace, and his voice was like the roar of many waters. In his right hand he held seven stars, from his mouth came a sharp two-edged sword, and his face was like the sun shining in full strength.

When I saw him, I fell at his feet as though dead. But he laid his right hand on me, saying, "Fear not, I am the first and the last, and the living one. I died, and behold I am alive forevermore, and I have the keys of Death and Hades. Write therefore the things that you have seen, those that are and those that are to take place after this. As for the mystery of the

> seven stars that you saw in my right hand, and the seven golden lampstands, the seven stars are the angels of the seven churches, and the seven lampstands are the seven churches."
>
> (Revelation 1:9–20)

The vision of heaven is always the vision of Jesus, the Son of Man, with everyone else, angels included, relative to Him. The problem for us is that we operate by faith and are blind to heaven-with-Jesus. Our loved ones with Jesus see Him continually. We do not see Him, nor do we see them as they really are, in joyful harmony with Him. But because of God's revelation there are sympathetic eschatological vibrations in our worship.

While we live in hope, the resurrection, our psalms, hymns, and spiritual songs stretch the fabric of our dimension thin so that we can hear the voices "further up and further in." This is good when I think of how close my sainted children actually are. It is a bit much when I have to acknowledge that God could take Kara or Daniel or our grandchildren there at any time. I've felt then that music can make heaven feel too close. Almost too accessible.

Walter Wangerin writes, "The singing undid me altogether. Music destroys me."[6] Though I have been playing trumpet every church festival since age ten, after Kyleigh died I could not play for almost a full year. I told the Lord quietly that if He took Stephan away, I would never play music for Him again. But now I believe that the music God has given me puts my wife and me in concert with our children—our children here and our children in heaven.

How much farther do I have to go? I cannot tell you. It is now February. It is raining at the cemetery today. Rain and snow, like God's Word.

Epiphany passes, Lent begins soon. I'm struck by the thought that we should skip Lent this year and get right to Easter. I would start my February Easter sermon with Paul's resurrection words,

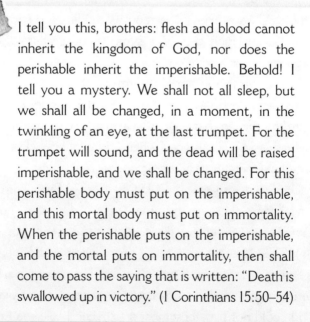

I tell you this, brothers: flesh and blood cannot inherit the kingdom of God, nor does the perishable inherit the imperishable. Behold! I tell you a mystery. We shall not all sleep, but we shall all be changed, in a moment, in the twinkling of an eye, at the last trumpet. For the trumpet will sound, and the dead will be raised imperishable, and we shall be changed. For this perishable body must put on the imperishable, and this mortal body must put on immortality. When the perishable puts on the imperishable, and the mortal puts on immortality, then shall come to pass the saying that is written: "Death is swallowed up in victory." (I Corinthians 15:50–54)

I would play my trumpet. For my Kinsman-Redeemer. For my kin, with Him in heaven.

It feels colder standing by Kyleigh's grave today. These visits are becoming easier and harder, at the same time. Easier, because her Father's will to bring her to heaven is a far, far better thing than anything I could have done for her.

Harder, too. You remember the bronze marker with our names, Kyleigh's and mine on it? There are spaces for more markers. There are spaces for my wife and me. There is also one more.

It tears my heart, just mentioning the possibility, but here it is. Right next to Kyleigh's grave, we have left room for Stephan's.

I do not, not, *not* want to carry another small coffin to this place. I do not want to have to explain again to anyone, or to myself, how heavy with glory it is. No! Wouldn't Stephan's death be a violation of Your promise, God, not to let anything happen beyond what we are able to bear?

Stephan's doctors tell us that he will certainly need a liver transplant within a few years. Every unexplained pain, every deviation in his lab work, even gradual declines in his health make me plead with Jesus that He will not give me *two* reasons to come here and seek. My surviving children can bury my body and mark the place with my name, but don't make me bury another of my children!

Still. Two weeks ago Stephan came running out of his bedroom in the early morning dark to find me reading at the kitchen table. His face was pale. He was trembling. "What is it, Sport?" I stood up to reach for him. "I had a nightmare." He reached out and hugged the breath out of me. "Dad," he sobbed, "I thought you had died!"

How did he know? I wanted to die. All these years of being manhandled by God until I felt like nothing more than a spectator to my son's suffering. Then this dreadful year of impotence, watching Kyleigh suffering and dying. Isn't a father supposed to protect his daughter, keep her safe from harm? I just wanted to die, to sleep, no more.

But my son's Heimlich hug that morning brought me to life with Paul's words.

> I am hard pressed between the two. My desire
> is to depart and be with Christ, for that is
> far better. But to remain in the flesh is more
> necessary on your account. Convinced of this,
> I know that I will remain and continue with
> you all, for your progress and joy in the faith.
> (Philippians 1:23–25)

For the time being, I do not plan to be visiting the cemetery quite so often. Stephan is well enough for school, even for playing some basketball and Little League baseball. It is a time to read and a time to play, a time to mourn and a time to be happy for a beloved girl, bright-eyed and singing for her God, with Him in Paradise.

It is a time, a time of grace, for me to be a father. To be a father writing these thoughts of a daughter who is alive even though she died, thoughts of fathers and children whose excruciating suffering is outweighed by their never-ending glory in Christ. We will go out with joy and be led in peace together. The mountains and the hills will sing and the trees will clap for us. All because of the Father and His Son and His once-and-for-all suffering for us.

Selah. Pause, further crescendo. More to come.

CHAPTER 5

The Scream

A dying child gives life up willingly,
If he is loved and held while dying.
Triumphant innocence can smile upon
Such terrors as make gladiators scream.

— Calvin Miller, A Symphony in Sand[1]

One dismal Friday in November, I screamed and wailed as I cradled my teenaged son. I screamed because, like you, I love. Love, love for God and for my neighbor, has not been a natural feature of human nature ever since the time of the insurrection in Eden. So, what creates and sustains this emotional field? What accounts for the force of love in our lives? We love because God first loved us (1 John 4:19). On the one hand, we can know love intellectually and discuss it logically, as we do in catechism and Bible classes or college classrooms. On the other hand, we already *know* love by virtue of our loving relationships prior to those intellectual discussions.

93

It is 2:30 in the morning, a couple of weeks after Stephan's first liver transplant. Things are not going well. He has been sleeping only fitfully. A couple of minutes ago, he called out, "Dad!" and I woke up to hurry over to his bed. Just now I am holding his head while he is being sick. As I open my mouth to tell him for the umpteenth time how much I admire his tenacity and cheerful faith in all that he is going through, he lifts a thin arm mapped with black-blue-yellow bruises and trailing an IV line to pull my forehead to his, in order to say weakly, "Dad, I love you."

When a son tells his dad from a hospital bed "I love you" (or when the Father of us all declares from heaven, "This is my beloved Son, whom I love!") this love is incontestable.

We can lie with our words, but our feelings are our feelings. The problem, then, is how to be sure that we love rightly, something Saint Augustine addresses at length. But first, given that we are skeptical people in a skeptical age, we ought to be aware that there is a foundation on which our feeling of love is built. Love is more real than gravity and more enduring than even faith and hope. Love never, ever ends (1 Corinthians 13:8).

Emotion Recollected

Many of us are familiar with that oft-quoted line about "emotion recollected in tranquility," but do you know that Wordsworth was not urging us to reflect quietly on our emotions? In fact, he was explaining how effective, poetic writing originates in having a mood and *at the same time* contemplating the meaning of that long-term emotion or mood. He said that good poetry, with its power to evoke emotion, enables us to reenact our human feelings and in this way we come to know the objective, universal truth of life for ourselves. As Wordsworth wrote in his *Preface to Lyrical Ballads* this is the way that poetry brings us "truth which is its own testimony, which gives strength and divinity to the tribunal to which it appeals." The insight is much older than Wordsworth. It is a long-standing feature of the Christian tradition. These two aspects of our consciousness taken together, namely, having an emotional feeling plus thinking about it—provide the way that God normally carries the difficult truth of things into our hearts.

Saint Gregory the Great argued, *Veritas non cognoscitur nisi amatur*, "The truth is not known unless it is loved."[2] Truth is not a matter of our intellectual assent alone. We certainly do not manufacture the truth, but neither is it the case that the truth is merely an object out there somewhere. "I am the truth," God has told us in person (John 14:6). Jesus has not told us that He is the truth in order to provide us with another byte of information or an objective fact. He has told us this so that we know Him by loving Him. Unless we believe, we will not understand. Similarly, unless we love, we will neither believe nor understand.

This understanding of emotional feeling, especially the recognition that our emotional being is a necessary condition for knowledge of the truth, would be a helpful footnote to the Lord Holy Spirit's own definition of faith in the first verse of Hebrews 11, since it is not possible to hope without love. "Now faith is the assurance of things hoped for, the conviction of things not seen." Gravity is real, though invisible. It is much more the case with love.

Love is not merely an ephemeral emotion, as if it were an incidental feature of our biology. Love is not pathological. Love is the force of our lives. In the fifth century AD Augustine wrote in his *Confessions*, "My weight is my love."[3] This is antique physics, but an apropos metaphor. He is saying that, just as it is in the nature of a stone to fall toward the center of the earth, so it is in human nature to be drawn toward people and things by love. He speaks of a thing's intrinsic "ponderousness."

We moderns see it differently. Our scientific understanding is not nature-centered but field oriented. We see rocks falling toward the earth and objects being attracted to one another as a matter of gravity fields. I would update Augustine's metaphor by saying that love is the field within which my family and I are drawn and held together. It is, as well, the field within which we love God. My gravity is love.

> *It is afternoon as we sit together in the family room. There is a scale model A-10 Warthog half-assembled on the end table. It smells of Testors paint. We received welcome news just a few hours earlier. Stephan's doctors at Children's Hospital have a donated liver and Stephan is going to be having the transplant that he urgently needs. Without saying anything aloud, we both know what the good news for us has meant for another family. We are grateful beyond words. Stephan is tuckered out, even with the oxygen he is on, twenty-four hours a day.*
>
> *"Steph, it's great that we're finally going to get the transplant, but I want to say something. It's possible that something could go wrong and if it does, I want you to know something, okay? The time may come when, even for you, it's going to be too much to keep going. I want you to know that, if you have to go, it's okay with Mom and me. We have never known anyone who is more ready for heaven. Jesus has given you such faith and you've certainly fought the good fight . . . " My voice*

> *breaks and Stephan says, "It's okay, Dad, I know."*
> *We both sit quietly for a few minutes and then it's*
> *back to the A-10.*

Augustine's physics would lead us to say that love is an integral part of our nature as creatures made in the image of God. It will be more helpful and more accurate, given how profoundly Adam and Eve's sin mutated human nature, to say that, just as God's making and preserving work includes the maintenance of gravity fields, so God's redeeming and sanctifying work includes the maintenance of love. I translate the 1 John 4:19 passage as "We go on loving for this reason, first and foremost: *He loved us*." Our feeling of love, then, is our orientation within this field of creation and creatures, a living, moment-by-moment relationship that God created and still preserves. And so, we ought to love God with all our heart, soul, mind, and strength and then our neighbors and then ourselves (Mark 12:30–31). This orientation, utterly lost in that rebellion at the tree of knowledge, is restored to us in the Gospel. Simone Weil puts it this way: "All the *natural* movements of the soul are analogous to those of physical gravity. Grace is the only exception."[4]

Love is not, as some contemporary thinkers put it, "non-foundational." It is not a feature of being human that just happens to affect us, either a vestigial feature of our evolutionary past or a creation of modern society propped up by a romantic piety. It is a universal feature of the cosmos. The center of gravity for this field is Christ's cross. John's classic explanation of the actual source of our feeling of love springs from an epistle and a God-breathed Book oriented toward God, who first loved us in Christ. The apostle urges us to love one another inasmuch as this is our orientation in Christ (1 John). In short, then, love orients us toward God and thus toward one another. Love orients us in life. Love orients us in death.

I mean to say that our weeping and crying suits our being human and our being in Christ. Think of who it is that came to Lazarus's wake. As we declare in the Creed, He is of one substance with the Father. He is also of one substance with grieving humanity.[5] As Rilke paints it in his poetic meditation on the raising of Lazarus (John 11), Jesus approached Bethany that day

> Deeply troubled.
>> His eyes resolutely slitted
>> He asked where the grave was.
> He suffered.
>> As was clear to them His tears flowed,
>> and they crowded in full of curiosity.
> En route it struck Him as monstrous,
>> an appalling playful temptation . . .

Abruptly an all-consuming fire erupted
    in Him, such a counterargument
        against their fundamentalist distinctions,
        their being-in-death and being-in life
    that He was vengeance in every body part
as He commanded hoarsely, "Heave away the stone!"[6]

In our sermons, we often preach the humanity of Christ
sedately, as if He were truly human, but without genuine
passion. He wept for a reason. Why did He weep? He was
angry, tormented, appalled. As very God of very God He
could—and did!—do something about His grief. As a mere
human being, I cannot raise my dead. I can only weep and
listen anxiously for the last trumpet. In a word, I can only
lament. This is the proper work of a human being. As we
heard earlier from Luther, weeping is preferred to working
and suffering exceeds all doing. We are not so much homo
sapiens as we are *homo lamentes*.

When Stephan breathed his last that terrible Friday in
November, I screamed.

> *I am utterly aghast . . . here in his intensive care*
> *room . . . but this is not the time. This is not the time*
> *for anything at all, except to gaze into his brown*
> *eyes and be here for him with all my heart, soul, and*
> *mind. Stephan is in the last minutes of his fourteen*
> *years with us. Over the past three months, every*

surgery, every procedure that we have consented to has failed. The failures have prolonged his suffering. (Lord, how You have made him suffer. Eleison, oh, eleison. Have mercy, oh, have mercy.) Two liver transplants. Intubations. Transfusions. Dialysis. Exotic mixtures of gases for his deteriorating lungs. Cardio shock. Pain, sleeplessness, indignity upon indignity. More pain.

Paula is embracing his legs, one hand clutching my left arm. My right arm is falling asleep as I cradle our son's head. "We love you, Steph. . . . Tell Kyleigh that we love her. . . . To have you as our son . . ." His breathing slows as we stare at each other, face to face, one last time. Alarms chime; we have been told that there is nothing more that anyone can do for him. The cancer somehow touched off by his second transplant has raged through his body and infected his brain. Two of us weep as his chest stops moving. We are still looking into his eyes, but he is not here any longer. In this room, one floor from where his little sister passed on, our beloved son dies in our arms.

I howl.

THE PROBLEM OF SUFFERING

Angry, Tormented, Appalled

As you have noticed, I do not speak of my love for Stephan and Kyleigh in the past tense any more than I would speak of my love for my wife and surviving children as something over and done with. My love for each of my loved ones is a present reality. It has been my experience, however, that many people in my life have tried in various ways to get me to "move on" after the deaths of our children. When people around us urge us to get over our children's deaths they are being modern-day friends of Job. We ought not try to get over our grief. It is part of God's résumé for us.

I have explained that grief is love. This means that grief is a kind of care. It is *pathos*, not at all in the sense that it makes us "pathological" and in need of therapy to get healthy again, but in the traditional, pre-modern sense of something real that deeply affects us where we live. As pathos grief is not a detached intellectual appraisal of things, nor is it essentially a voluntary activity that originates in the will of the individual. It is an ongoing care in the sense of the Latin *cura*, meaning the constant, loving care one has for what is cared for. The grieving person is a curate whose sacred office is a preoccupation that colors his every occupation, whatever his day in, day out vocation may be.

Grief as care is an obsession, an attention—not to "mortality" or to "the human condition"—but *to a person* who is at the same time dearly loved and agonizingly absent. Grief is gravity. It is a gravity that bridges the event horizon of death. Grief is grief without our willing it to be so and before and after we interrogate it and try to think it through.

So, what about my screaming? You may want to tell me that this outburst was the result of my sinfulness. I do not for a second deny that I am a sinner, unclean in thought, word, and deed. This is both my inherited condition as well as something for which I am personally culpable. I daily sin much. It is also true that I object to what has happened to my children with every fiber of my being. Sometimes I have refused to pray to God about this. This refusal is sin and rebellion on my part for which I need absolution. I have also prayed to God while outraged and angry and furious with Him. These angry prayers are not sinful. In fact, they have often been prayers echoing Job and Psalms and the Prophets. Our screams and our prayers in the face of suffering and death are metaphysically proper *when they are directed to the Lord God*.

> *Here we are, in church for Stephan's visitation and funeral. There is an honor guard posted at his casket, young men and women rendering their final duty in Air Force dress blues and white gloves. We approach his casket and I reach out to touch his hair. "Oh, Stephan," I whisper. After a few*

minutes I stand with Paula, Kara, and Daniel—holding hands, arms around shoulders, weeping. When my dad comes up a bit later, he too is crying. He hugs me and says, chokingly, "I guess I'm going to see him first."

I find myself feeling positively furious. Abruptly it dawns on me. My father is probably right. But what it means for me is infuriating. It is very likely that I am not going to see Stephan again for over thirty or forty years. No!

It has been a decade since we last held Stephan in our arms, but I still feel the way I did that Friday afternoon in November. I often look at the crook of my right elbow and know it as a sacred place. Now I want to understand, if I can, what it means for me to feel the way I do, not just about Stephan's suffering and death, but how I feel toward his God.

My basic thought is to take a lesson from my feelings. I do not see this as an effort merely to report how my son's and daughter's deaths affected me while acknowledging that the experience will, of course, be different for every grieving parent. Just the opposite. My expectation is that the entire family of Adam and Eve feels this way as our children suffer and die. Our emotional states of love, grief, anguish, are, I am thinking, the ties that bind and relate us to our children and to one another. These ties are personal and honest, for they are immediate. We are thinking beings, as Descartes famously wrote, but in a more basic sense we are feeling and loving beings as well.

I love my children, my daughter on earth and my daughter in heaven, my son who is with us and my son who is already with Jesus in glory. I love their mother, my beloved wife. This love does not originate in me. It originates, like water constantly bubbling up from an artesian spring, in Christ and His cross. Remember John's first epistle.

Why Do We Weep

Why, then, did I scream at Stephan's death? Why do I still sob whenever I think about his death and Kyleigh's, as I am doing right now, writing this chapter and re-collecting again my feelings at the suffering my children had to face? I was shouting "No" then. I am still shouting "No" today, in the aftermath of their deaths. There is more to this than emotional release; there is emotional truth here as well.

People, believers and unbelievers alike, weep at funerals. We weep at the death of our children and loved ones. We feel the significance of what has happened, but the cause of our weeping is different. As in Dickinson poem states, parting is all we know of heaven. Or is it?

Meaningfulness is always part and parcel of our griev-ing and weeping. This in itself is no guarantee that we can or will discern a valid reason for our grief. Nevertheless, grieving is an experience that is never without a felt meaning. We see this irrefragable meaningfulness in our human experience of grief, for example, in Tolstoy's description of the death of Prince Andrei in *War and Peace*. Every mourner in this scene wept for a reason. As they paid their respects at Andrei's coffin, Nikolushka wept because he was heartbroken and baffled. Sonya wept because "he was no more." The aged count wept because he knew that he would die soon. Natasha and Marya wept because of their pious and reverent feelings in the presence of death.[7]

Every mourner *weeps* in Tolstoy's narrative—the exact same Russian word is used seven consecutive times here, no cognates[8]—but each mourner weeps for a different reason. Not one of us who grieves feels that his weeping is mere lachrymation, a flow of tears; our weeping is always for a reason. We may have many different reasons. Nevertheless, grief as a conscious experience is intentional. That is, grieving is always about someone, about what is happening. Grieving is about someone and about our separation from that person. We never just grieve, we always *grieve for*. And this is as far as we can go in learning from grief per se.

As we have just seen, it is the case that not everyone grieves for the same reason. It is rather as Paul reminds us of the apostles' informed understanding "about those who are asleep, that you may not grieve as others do who have no hope" (1 Thessalonians 4:13). As with Jesus' death and resurrection, so too with those who have fallen asleep in Him. With Tolstoy's description of weeping still fresh in mind, let me mention a second depiction of grief from Russian literature, this one from Dostoevsky. In *The Brothers Karamazov* one of the Karamazov brothers, Alyosha, has just learned from the lips of his spiritual mentor and friend that this faithful and beloved friend is going to die soon. Do you remember how Alyosha's mentor attentively asks what's wrong and then reminds his young seminary student that Christ is with him, that He will keep Alyosha in the grieving that lies just ahead? Echoing Jesus' refrain to let people of this world follow their dead, Elder Zosimov tells Alyosha to keep Christ since Christ will keep him.[9]

What accounts for the difference between the individual, idiosyncratic reasons for weeping among Prince Andrei's mourners on the one hand and Alyosha's weeping on the other? The difference is Christ. I do not say, "The difference is Christianity," but "The difference is *Christ*," so that we do not miss the crucial center of gravity. God's love for us in Christ is the foundation of love—remember, we love now because, first and foremost, He loved us— and love, in turn, is the stuff, the substance of grief. As I mentioned, there is more to this than simply the shout of "No." There is the matter of what it is that I believe, the substance of the faith in and from Christ that lies beneath that shout. When we believers weep, we weep to God.

The critical question, then, is whether our grief-love is ultimately grounded in the love of Christ or whether our love goes to ground in persons whom we love absolutely, apart from God altogether. In other words, is it just that two of my children are gone and I feel bad about this, or is there a reason why I *ought* to feel the grief I feel?

The grief of a Christian believer is different in kind from the grief of a disbeliever. Grieving is what it is, an experience of love. All men grieve. But the grieving of the believer is different because of his hope for the future in terms of his relation with Christ. Recall 1 Thessalonians 4:13–18. We weep to the God who wept for Lazarus and is on the move toward the graves of our loved ones this very minute.

The difference is brought about by God's living revelation of Christ in His Word. The meaning of the feeling of meaningfulness cannot be puzzled out; rather, it is delivered by God's revelation. The event horizon of death will be bridged at last when God "will bring with Him those who have fallen asleep in Jesus." Jesus loves me, this I know, for the Bible tells me so. Ultimately He will wipe away every tear from our eyes (Revelation 7:17). But for the time being, we weep to God.

There is more. The believer has in hand (or in his heart of his being, if you will) evidence of the reunion to come in the present reality of Christ and His care for him. That is to say, during the in-between time of separation from those we love, the risen Jesus is Himself the substantiation of our hope. He is the evidence of things not seen (Hebrews 11:1). This evidence is reintroduced to the believer day in and day out in the Sacraments. Through the Word, the Supper, Baptism, and Absolution, God affects the gravity of grief with His grace.

Notwithstanding our confidence in this hoped-for reunion, our faith does not eliminate our finitude. In other words, our faith in Christ does not allow us to escape our temporality and the very real experience of separation from those we love when they die. We who grieve remain for now on this side of the event horizon of death. We believers grieve, but we never grieve in absolute isolation. We weep to the God who wept for us, as one of us.

Grieving as human beings do, we continue to feel the gravity of death. Grieving as Christ's members, we experience in addition the grace of Christ's redemptive work *pro nobis*, or on our behalf, as we say in Lutheran theology. As Luther puts it in his commentary on Isaiah 53,

> This is the second part of our understanding and justification, to know that Christ suffered and was cursed and killed, but FOR US. It is not enough to know the matter, the suffering, but it is necessary to know its function.[10]

The difference between the grief of the Christian and those who grieve without hope in Christ is *Christ*. Because of His Resurrection, that is, the rising from death of the One who is acquainted with grief (Isaiah 53:3–4), the gravity of grief as experienced by believers, whether on the first Easter or by us in the twenty-first century, is modulated and sanctified by grace.

The thing is that I cannot spend the next thirty years or more sitting in sackcloth and ashes, weeping, can I? There are memorials to be constructed while I wait in grieving hope.

CHAPTER 6

In Memoriam

At this waypoint in grief I am bereft
            of understanding,
so this massive darkness crushes me flat.
You however are another matter. Make
            Yourself grievously heavy, tunnel in!
Then and only then will you really lay
            Your hand on me
And I will really place my scream on You.

— Rainer Maria Rilke,
"A Book for the Hours of Prayer"[1]

My memorial for my son began with readying the uniform that he would wear for his burial, two days before his funeral.

Here I am. In Stephan's bedroom, the day after his death. My God. At this moment, his body, overwritten with scars from his heart surgery and fresh wounds from his liver transplants, and more, is being transported from the hospital to the funeral home. It is Saturday and so I wonder in passing how God the Father felt on the Saturday after His Son's death. But this inspires no pious meditation on my part; I remain utterly appalled at what He has done. After all these years of hospitals and surgeries, all the promise of a young man with such a determined, faithful nature—there is practically no space to breathe. My God, why? *How could You? He was only fourteen.*

*Paula and I will go in a few hours to finalize arrangements and to compose an obituary for our child. Again. But now I am at home, sitting in his room, among the clouds; clouds his mom had painted on the walls and sewn on the blankets she sewed for him when he was alive (*when he was alive. . .*). Without looking over my right shoulder, I know every detail of the model B-17 hanging from the ceiling by the window. I know the titles of the books under his bed and exactly where to find his copy of the Uniform Manual. It is in a shelf at the back of his closet. On the floor of the closet there are also, I know, three bags of his things that we brought home from the hospital last night. In one of them is his Bible with Acts 14:22, his chosen confirmation verse, carefully underlined by him in black ink. "We must go through many hardships to enter the kingdom of God" (NIV).*

So. I have laid out his dress uniform on his favorite rocking chair. Double-check the alignment. Polish the devices. Scrutinize the blues for lint. Everything is already meticulous, of course. He had it all shipshape months ago, good-to-go for his next squadron meeting, but this final inspection is something I owe him. Something to memorize, I think distantly, something to memorialize *my son. This is hardly a private memorial, of course. His mom sewed and pressed this uniform over the years. Others first pinned these rank and insignia on his lapel. In the hospital a month earlier a veteran from his squadron gave Stephan the paratrooper wings from his own service in the military. He told me that these stay with Stephan, so I button the wings into his blouse pocket. In this week after Veteran's Day, he is being readied for burial in his country's uniform, the uniform worn by so many others at their funerals. His flight cap, I notice, smells like Stephan. I inhale and tell myself to remember.*

I cannot bear the absence, nor will I let any of my tears stain his uniform. One more detail: these solo wings that I have been saving for him. I consider briefly pinning them on the left breast, just above his ground team badge, but the truth is that Stephan was hospitalized shortly before he was to

> *fly solo. I can almost hear him telling me, "Thanks,*
> *Dad, but I didn't earn those, so don't pin them on,*
> *okay?" Okay, Sarge. I will give these to the funeral*
> *director to place in your hands. That seems fitting*
> *and right, on a number of levels.* In memoriam,
> *my son.*

Stephan loved the Civil Air Patrol. Since World War II, CAP has been the auxiliary of the U.S. Air Force where adult seniors and teenagers (called "cadets") practice search and rescue, learn about aerospace, and train in moral leadership. Stephan was a CAP cadet and so was buried in Air Force blues. Scores of seniors and cadets attended his funeral in uniform. Members of his squadron served as honor guard and pallbearers at church and graveside. A lifelong friend of mine played taps at his interment. It was my task to prepare my son's uniform with its grade, ribbons, and rating badges for his burial.

Abraham Heschel says, "The world consists, not of things, but of tasks."[2] This has helped me to see my life as a place of tasks. I can even be specific about the type of tasks that make up my life. My world has come to consist, not of tasks and livelihood, but of memorials. Memorial-building has become my vocation.

This Do in Remembrance

As I am sure you understand, I do want to memorialize Stephan by doing things in his memory. For example, I have continued my service as an officer in CAP as a living memorial to him. Now and then in my moral leadership lessons I mention Cadet Master Sergeant Stephan Schulz as an example of what my cadets have come to know as "master sergeants of integrity." Since his death, I have taken flying lessons and soloed. I became qualified to fly search and rescue missions as an air crew member. I teach, serve, and mentor other young CAP cadets, all in his memory. This impulse seems to have its genesis in me, in my desire to do something significant for my late son. But this is not what I mean by living out my life as a memorial.

With the poet Rainer Maria Rilke I confess that I don't have much knowledge yet in grief, but to live *in memoriam*. This, I keep discovering, is in fact a matter of God's grace and not merely a matter of my determination. My life is lived in the genre of lamentation. This is how I give voice to my scream of grief.

> *Lament isn't an inarticulate wail. Lament notices details, images, and relationships. Pain can become poetry. Poetry is our most personal use of words. It is our way of entering deeply into the experience and bringing beauty out of it.*

> *Lament is deeply private, but it can also be deeply*
> *public. . . . Lament keeps us connected with reality,*
> *and with the deepest of all realities: God.* [3]

Of course, I will not let myself or others forget my son, but my life of memorial lamentation rests on a deeper reality. As José Ortega Y Gasset puts it, "When we meditate, our mind has to be kept at full tension; it is a painful and integral effort."[4] This is so because, as Ortega explains, when we meditate we shove off from our superficial notions of things and launch out into the depths. Out of the depths, I cry. Out of the depths, I cry to Thee. Sometimes profound, sometimes superficial, I cry.

Do you know the *Paradiso*, the portrayal of Dante's visit to heaven in his *Divine Comedy*? There it is Beatrice, the long-lost love of the middle-aged poet's life, who guides him into the presence of God. I used to recommend to my students that they think of the entire poem as a poetic version of Thomas Aquinas's philosophy, organized according to Aristotelian logic.

John Gardner, a well-known American author and creative writing teacher, says that my advice was superficial. Dante, he argues, discovered a new mode of thought, no less, in the course of thinking and writing about heaven. This new way of thinking freed him from what Gardner calls "the ferule of logic." It works this way: As we can see in the closing stanzas of the poem's first part, the *Purgatorio*, and throughout the *Paradiso*, in his writing Dante continually asked himself—not primarily what Aquinas or Aristotle would say about his writing—but rather what *Beatrice*, Dante's first love, would say. It seems to me, then, that the entire poem is, at one level, a literary memorial to Beatrice. Professor Gardner adds, "Most of us, I hope, have had some child or spouse or friend like Beatrice, someone who by his very nature, his seemingly innate goodness and intelligence, makes us uncomfortably conscious of our lies when we lie."[5] I have had such a child. I still do, with Jesus in heaven.

> *The liver transplant has failed. What has been evident in Stephan's condition is now confirmed by the lab numbers and his doctor. A matter of weeks after the transplant, he is going to need still another liver in order to live. "Steph, wake up. Mom and I have to talk over something with you." I have in mind a logical explanation. I am going to explain to him that, just as Paula and I have to trust his doctors to know what has to be done, he will have to trust their judgment too. Of course, he already senses what is coming. "But I don't* want *another transplant," he says. I launch into my analogy. "You know, Sport, how you trust Mom and me. . . ." That's as far as he lets me go. "Okay, Dad, it's okay then," and he puts his head on his pillow, goes back to sleep.*

I am a memorial and Stephan is my Beatrice. His good and intelligent character that I so miss is a gift of God, nothing less. You remember how Stephan hugged me hard that morning after his sister's death and said that he had dreamt my death? I did want to die; it was the thought of Stephan that stopped me. While I screamed at what my family had to face, Stephan faced his own death with a triumphant innocence. God saw to it that, in such a brief time of grace, he lived up to his namesake, the first Christian martyr. In the case of our Stephan, his martyrdom was quieter, but all the more intense for us because of its economy. To be a martyr entails more than a dramatic death scene. To be a martyr is to be a witness to the truth in life and then, as part of the whole, in death. It means to live with integrity. Martyrs are memorials in the flesh. In this way, they are memorials to what is excellent and praiseworthy, the very things that the apostle Paul, in his letter to the Philippians, urges us to keep thinking about.

Thermopylae and Memorial Day

In an historical note prefacing his *Gates of Fire: An Epic Novel of the Battle of Thermopylae*, Steven Pressfield sketches out the situation between the invading Persian King Xerxes and the factious Greeks in 480 BC. He recounts Herodotus's report that the Spartans fought the Persians "with bare hands and teeth."

> The Spartans and their Thespian allies died to the last man, but the standard of valor they set by their sacrifice inspired the Greeks to rally and, in that fall and spring, defeat the Persians at Salamis and Plataea and preserve the beginnings of Western democracy and freedom from perishing in the cradle.[6]

Pressfield reminds us of the two memorials that are at Thermopylae still today.

It may be that epics depict things as they never were, in largely idealistic ways, but those two memorials inspire the best in us nonetheless. I have seen the tears and the resolve in the faces of hundreds of CAP cadets and officers to whom I have spoken of the Spartan memorials while teaching them the U.S. Air Force's core value of integrity.

I realize that my son's example will not inspire others on the scale of the Spartans' sacrifice at Thermopylae, but this is hardly the point. Stephan is not himself the story; he is part of the never-ending story, as is his little sister. His life and death do not memorialize Stephan, like a statue standing heroically on its own, but Stephan in relationship to his sisters and brother, to us, his parents, to his friends from CAP and at church, and to his God. I have not come to praise Stephan nor to make of him a virtual monument, but to call to remembrance *who he is in relationship to Christ*, who first loved us.

The tenacity of this reality shows up in the way we each made our lives memorials to Stephan. His older sister, Kara, joined the Air Force in order to put on the uniform for service to her country, in large part as a personal testimony to her brother. She memorialized his service with her service. Daniel, Stephan's younger brother, memorialized Stephan's faithfulness and quiet determination by adding it to his own substantial resolve. Stephan's determination is one reason that Daniel set about being a four-sport varsity athlete in high school. He got into the habit of writing Stephan's name on his shoes and then went on to earn varsity positions as a starter in football, basketball, track, and baseball. Paula and I have each found ways to do things in our teaching, writing, and living *in memoriam* to Stephan and Kyleigh.

> *Heel to shiny heel, twenty-some teenagers and a half-dozen adults are standing at attention in Air Force blues, enframing two graves. Both markers bear my name, one with pink flowers in its bronze vase, one with red, white, and blue flowers and an American flag. It is Memorial Day at Wisconsin Memorial Park. These are members of Stephan's*

CAP squadron. They assemble every year to render honors. Here, of all places.

Three of the senior officers knew Stephan person-ally; the teenage cadets know him through me. "This is the grave of one of our own," I say. "Thank you for coming. Most of you heard me tell the story of Thermopylae at encampment last summer and the inspiring example of the Spartans' sacrifice. We have just been part of a ceremony to keep alive the memory of the ultimate sacrifice made by people in the military so that we would have the freedom to assemble here today and the freedom to worship and live as we do. Now, it is one thing—a noble and honorable thing beyond measure—to make such a sacrifice for others, but this is only half the lesson of Memorial Day. What is important now is what we do with this expensive, expensive freedom in order to be worthy of it. How will you live your own life? One example of faith and life that you may want to take to heart is that of Cadet Master Sergeant Stephan Schulz, my sainted son. . . ."

Not at Rest . . . Until

This is the closest I can come to a conclusion to my meditation on the suffering and death of my children. In his comments on 2 Samuel and the life's story of King David, Eugene Peterson, Bible translator and pastor, says, "There's a great temptation in making a conclusion to a story to make things tidy. . . . But tidiness does violence both to Scripture and to life."[7] I have tried to avoid this temptation overall, but I do realize that the very activity of writing suggests a settled-ness or tidiness that I do not have. Or rather, that I do not have and hold every day. Triumph and perfectionism I have none, but what I have, I have given you. What I have shared is an aspect of what is known as Luther's theology of the cross.[8]

I can well understand that you may be expecting a book like this to help you to be completely at peace with your own losses, now that you've read it through. I hope it will help; it is replete with God's Word and Christ's Gospel, which are always effective—but even the Gospel doesn't give us absolute rest *as long as we are away from home in this vale of tears*. It can and it does bring us the Good News of Jesus, the rest for our souls, but we still experience anger and anxiety.

Our desire, to put it abstractly for a moment, is to see reality whole and our place in it as secure as can be. Medieval thinkers understood love this way. We feel love as desire when the beloved is absent; we feel love as joy when the beloved is present. Now, Jesus is always present. His face is always toward me, but (sinner that I am) mine is not always toward Him. When I am listening to Paul's cadence of "rejoices" in his epistle to the Philippians and all the rest of Holy Scripture, I rejoice. But two of my loved ones are still absent *to me*. My joy is not complete. It cannot be, until God grants us all a blessed reunion in heaven.

Jesus, the incarnate God, is the origin and the goal of everything, as we read in Colossians 1. This means that Stephan and Kyleigh are experiencing joy upon joy in His presence. But for all the truth and comfort of the Gospel, I cannot stay centered as I ought, "looking to Jesus, the founder and perfecter of our faith" (Hebrews 12:2).

A week before passing into the joy of God's presence, shortly after his last Holy Communion, Stephan managed to sit up in his hospital bed and ask, "Dad, am I going to die?"

"It's possible, Sport."

Stephan nodded an okay and went back to sleep. I did not. A few days later, he fell asleep in Jesus. But I have not. I keep waking up in the shadow-lands. Our temporal existence this side of that event horizon, even in light of the eternal Gospel, accounts for our doubts, our anxiety, our disquiet.

The classic passage on this anxiety or *Angst* that we keep feeling is found in the opening paragraph of Augustine's *Confessions*: "You [that is, the Lord God] have made us for Yourself and our heart is disquieted until it finds itself quieted in You." I paraphrase it this way: "Our heart is *Angst*-ridden and not at home unless and until we find ourselves at home in You." This is the reason that Jesus taught us to pray "Deliver us!" and the reason that Luther taught us to be sure that we are ready to die whenever we pray this petition of the Lord's Prayer. The divine reply to our anxiety is Jesus' promise, "My peace I give to you. Not as the world gives do I give to you. Let not your hearts be troubled, neither let them be afraid" (John 14:27). So, when our children suffer and die, we have our anxiety. And, we have Christ, not our own thinking and resolve to rely on, but rather His Word.

> For My thoughts are not your thoughts,
>> neither are your ways My ways,
>>> declares the LORD.
> For as the heavens are higher than the earth,
>> so are My ways higher than your ways
>> and My thoughts than your thoughts.
>
> For as the rain and the snow come
>> down from heaven
>> and do not return there but water the earth,
> making it bring forth and sprout,
>> giving seed to the sower and bread to the eater,
> so shall My word be that goes out
>> from My mouth;

it shall not return to Me empty,
but it shall accomplish that which I purpose,
    and shall succeed in the thing for which I sent it.

For you shall go out in joy and be led forth in peace;
the mountains and the hills before you
    shall break forth into singing,
    and all the trees of the field shall clap their hands.

(Isaiah 55:8–12)

A father and his children, our Father and His children. Here am I and the children You have given me.

Amen and *selah*.

Epilogue

Prayers and Poems Written by Sufferers

St. Ephraim Syrus (ca. AD 306–373) wrote over eighty-five funeral hymns. This is one which he subtitled "Motives for Restraining Sorrow."

On the Death of a Child

Oh my son, tenderly loved!
Whom grace fashioned
In his mother's womb,
And divine goodness completely formed.
He appeared in the world
Suffering like a flower,
And death put forth a heat
More fierce than the sun,
And scattered its leaves
And withered it, that it ceased to be.

I fear to weep for thee,
Because I am instructed
That the Son of the Kingdom hath removed thee
To His bright habitation.

Nature, in its fondness,
Disposes me to tears,
Because, my son, of thy departure.
But when I remember the bright abode
To which they have led thee,
I fear lest I should defile
The dwelling-place of the King
By weeping, which is adverse to it;
And lest I should be blamed,
For coming to the region of bliss
With tears which belong to sadness;
I will therefore rejoice,
Approaching with my pure offering.

The sound of thy sweet notes
Once moved me and caught mine ear,
And caused me much to wonder;
Again my memory listens to it,
And is affected by the tones
And harmonies of thy tenderness.
But when my spirit groans aloud

On account of these things,
My judgment recalls me,
And listens with admiration
To the voices of those who live on high;
To the song of the spiritual ones
Who cry aloud, Hosannah!
At thy marriage festival.[1]

During the winter of Kyleigh's final hospitalization, one of our seminary students who was teaching a number of my confirmation classes translated and sent us this prayer. The original prayer is by Nickolaus Haas (1665–1715). The translator is Ib Van Meyer.

> Almighty God, loving Father. You did not speak to Abraham alone when you said: I am your God and the God of your seed after you. However, you also assured us through your apostle that this promise would appear to us and our children. Therefore, do not be angry as I now dare to converse with you, and to pour out my prayer and groans for my sick child in your bosom.
>
> Lord! She is your creation and your handi-work, you made her in the womb, presented

her with body and soul, and gave life and blessings to her. You brought her to the light of the world, and received her in Holy Baptism as your child, also keeping her in your grace until this time. Now, accordingly, may you take control in her great weakness. Oh! Do not consider her sins, in which she was conceived and born, and with which she has trodden on your holy law in her life. Be merciful according to your great goodness, alleviate her pain and sickness, and if it is your will, make her healthy soon. For, Lord, she stands in your hand and power, restore her to complete health, and you will do this, if you find that she is beneficial to your honor, my welfare, and your own blessedness.

However, if you proceed differently with her according to your holy advice, that either she lies still longer in her sickbed, or she should die early, then not my will, but your will be done, which is always the best. Lord Jesus, you dear Lamb of God, who bore the sins of the world! Look at this poor lamb, which you have bought to be your own with the all-precious ransom. Wake her and purify her from all her sins with your guiltless blood. Strengthen her through your Holy Spirit in true faith to yourself and your service, in Christian patience under your cross, which you laid on her, and in the hope of your gracious help. It was pleasing to you that I should pull back and see this child in your terror, as she grew through your blessing year after year in all Christian purity, and so I want to praise your name always and forever. Lord, speak now a word, so that she will become healthy and alive! However, if you decide, take her to yourself through a blessed death (as you have more power and might concerning this than I). Thus I am therefore content, and know you will present her soul as a spirit of perfect righteousness in heaven through your holy angel; the sick body will be made to resemble your glorious body on that day—the resurrection of the righteous, dressed with your blessed immortality.

God the Holy Spirit, you Spirit of adoption and God of all comfort, fill my sad soul and my sick child with your mighty comfort. Help her weakness through your heavenly might, plead for her before God with unspeakable sighs. Also, grant me the grace that I throw myself under, obedient to, the will of God, humbly under your strong hand, waiting with a quiet spirit the end of this sickness, saying nothing but this: You are the Lord, do what is pleasing. I have until now seen the blessedness of God in this child—the blessedness of God and a godly character, for she obeys you, that she may both produce and dedicate to you in life and death. She will be taken from my kisses and arms through death, but you are placing her in the kiss of your grace, and she will be complete in heaven by the breast of your comfort. She will pour forth joy eternally, the fullness and loving ways of your justice.

Amen! Lord, Trinity, speak to my prayer and supplication your Amen. Yes, yes, thus it will happen. Amen.

It is my hope that *The Problem of Suffering* will bring courage and a taste of God's love to those of you who have brothers and sisters who are suffering—or already in heaven. The following poem was written for Kyleigh by her sister Kara (then 13 years old) one year after Kyleigh's death.

Sleep On, Sweet Sister

Fair and sweet, sister dear,
Now that nearly a year
Of sleepless nights
You have borne,
You have left your sterile crib
To sleep,
Safely slumber
So securely.

Though glad I am you now can slumber,
My heart aches that you must sleep
Before I know you
Or you know me.
I now implore that you
Not forget me
As you sleep on.
Me you must remember
And wait for me you must,
And I'll be home soon.
Until then,
Fair and sweet, sister dear,
Sleep on.
Sleep on.
Sleep on in peaceful rest.

I had been working on the following song for another occasion, but while preparing his Civil Air Patrol uniform for his visitation, I rethought the refrain and knew that this hymn was meant for Stephan. The tunes on which the hymn is based were first a soundtrack in my mind and in my throat. The poetry followed from the music, emerging from familiar biblical vocabulary and also from the Tolkien epic that Stephan and I loved to read together, especially during the long nights of his suffering when we waited like watchmen for the morning, like watchmen for the morning. Over the weekend between his death and his funeral, my friend and colleague Dr. James Nowack wrote out a setting for the hymn and then directed our entire college choir in singing it for the service.

Now, Faithful Warrior

Among the fray an arm is raised,
A gaze uplifted to the sky.
Amid the din, the Captain's voice.
Our lives are pledged, we make reply:

> Soon, faithful warriors, soon the rest!
> This day—the agony. This day, the test.
> But coming's the feast that knows no fast!
> Soon, faithful warriors, soon the rest.

Self-minded foe, his weapons dire,
his hordes long-lived to keep the siege.
Yet we have seen and still we bear
the coming of the LORD, our liege:

> Soon, faithful warriors, soon the rest!
> This day—the agony. This day, the test.
> But coming's the feast that knows no fast!
> Soon, faithful warriors, soon the rest.

Our standard points all to the prize
through warfare fierce and campaign long,
a crown of gold, a place by Him.
Come, voice with us this triumph song:

> Now, faithful warrior, now the rest!
> Finished the agony, finished the test.
> Beginning the feast that knows no fast!
> Now, faithful warrior, now, now your rest.

for Stephan's Christian funeral, 16 November 1998
by Gregory P. Schulz
to the tunes of Gift of Love by Hal H. Hopson (stanza)
and Slane, an Irish folk song (refrain).

Lament

He has made my teeth grind on gravel,
>   and made me cower in ashes;
my soul is bereft of peace;
>   I have forgotten what happiness is;
so I say, "My endurance has perished;
>   so has my hope from the LORD."
Remember my affliction and my wanderings,
>   the wormwood and the gall!
My soul continually remembers it
>   and is bowed down within me.
But this I call to mind,
>   and therefore I have hope:
The steadfast love of the LORD never ceases;
>   his mercies never come to an end;
they are new every morning;
>   great is your faithfulness.
"The LORD is my portion," says my soul,
>   "therefore I will hope in Him."
The LORD is good to those who wait for Him,
>   to the soul who seeks Him.
It is good that one should wait quietly
>   for the salvation of the LORD.

It is good for a man that he bear
>> the yoke in his youth.
Let him sit alone in silence
>> when it is laid on him;
let him put his mouth in the dust—
>> there may yet be hope;
let him give his cheek to the one who strikes,
>> and let him be filled with insults.
For the Lord will not
>> cast off forever,
but, though He cause grief, He will have compassion
>> according to the abundance of His steadfast love;
for He does not willingly afflict
>> or grieve the children of men.
To crush underfoot
>> all the prisoners of the earth,
to deny a man justice
>> in the presence of the Most High,
to subvert a man in his lawsuit,
>> the Lord does not approve.
Who has spoken and it came to pass,
>> unless the Lord has commanded it?
Is it not from the mouth of the Most High
>> that good and bad come? (Lamentations 3:16–38)

Notes

Foreword

1. AE 31:53.

Preface

1. C. S. Lewis, *The Problem of Pain* (New York: Macmillan Publishing Company, 1962), 10.

Chapter 1

1. AE 14:145.
2. Nicholas Wolterstorff, *Lament for a Son* (Grand Rapids: Eerdmans, 1987), 96.

Chapter 2

1. This is a component of my regular presentation at DOXOLOGY retreats for pastors who minister to suffering souls in their congregations and communities.
2. John Milton, *Complete Poetry* (Garden City, New York: Doubleday & Co., 1971), 252.
3. C. S. Lewis, *The Problem of Pain* (New York: Macmillan Publishing Company, 1962), 10.
4. Nicholas Wolterstorff, *Lament for a Son* (Grand Rapids: Eerdmans, 1987), 97.
5. Kenneth Surin, "Taking Suffering Seriously," in *The Problem of Evil: Selected Readings*, Michael Peterson, ed. (Notre Dame, IN: University of Notre Dame Press, 1992), 339.
6. AE 14:140.

7. Martin Luther, *Sermons of Martin Luther* (Grand Rapids: Baker Book House, 1983), 1:311.

8. *Sermons of Martin Luther*, 1:312.

9. John Meyer, *Ministers of Christ* (Milwaukee: Northwestern Publishing House, 1963, 2011), 293.

10. C. S. Lewis, *A Grief Observed* (New York: Bantam Books, 1988), 5.

11. Harold Kushner, *When Bad Things Happen to Good People* (New York: Avon Books, 1981), 43.

12. William Edwards, "On the Physical Death of Jesus Christ," *Journal of the American Medical Association* (March 1986): 1463. See the fuller discussion of Jesus' death in Gerard Joseph Stanley Sr., *He Was Crucified: Reflections on the Passion of Christ* (St. Louis: Concordia, 2009), 164.

13. AE 4:92, 94.

14. Søren Kierkegaard, *Fear and Trembling: The Sickness unto Death* (Garden City, NY: Doubleday & Co., 1954), 39.

15. Lewis, *The Problem of Pain*, 144.

16. George Herbert (1593–1633), *The Temple: Sacred Poems and Private Ejaculations* (1633). Source for this setting: *The Poetical Works Of George Herbert*, ed. George Gilfillan (Edinburgh: James Nichol, 1853).

Chapter 3

1. AE 35:30–31.

2. C. S. Lewis, *A Grief Observed* (New York: Bantam Books, 1988), 29–30.

3. Donald Deffner, *At the Death of a Child: Words of Comfort and Hope* (St. Louis: Concordia, 1993), 10.

4. Sheldon Vanauken, *A Severe Mercy* (New York: Bantam Books, 1979), 235–36.

5. *Christian Worship: A Lutheran Hymnal* (Milwaukee: Northwestern Publishing House), 32.

6. See Phillip Cary, *Outward Signs: The Powerlessness of External Things in Augustine's Thought* (Oxford University Press, 2008), Preface.

Chapter 4

1. J. R. R. Tolkien, *The Return of the King* (Boston: Houghton Mifflin Company, 1987), 384.

2. J. R. R. Tolkien, *The Tolkien Reader* (New York: Ballantine Books, 1966), 79.

3. C. S. Lewis, *The Chronicles of Narnia: The Last Battle* (New York:

Macmillan Publishing Co., First Collier Books Edition, 1970), 183.

4. *The Chronicles of Narnia: The Last Battle*, 183–84.

5. T. S. Eliot, *The Complete Poems and Plays* (New York: Harcourt, Brace & World, Inc., 1971), 129.

6. Walter Wangerin, *The Manger Is Empty: Stories in Time* (Zondervan-Harper, San Francisco, 1989), 64.

Chapter 5

1. Calvin Miller, *A Symphony in Sand* (Word Publishing, 1996), 64.

2. See Patrick Henry Reardon, "Truth Is Not Known Unless It Is Loved" in *Books and Culture* (September / October 1998).

3. Augustine (Maria Boulding, trans.), *Confessions* 13,9 (Hyde Park, NY: New City Press, 1997), 348.

4. Simone Weil (Emma Craufurd, trans.), *Gravity and Grace* (New York: Routledge, 1997), 1.

5. See, for example, Martin Chemnitz (J. A. O. Preus, trans.), *The Two Natures in Christ* (St. Louis: Concordia, 1578, 1971), p. 171: "The hypostatic union of the two natures of Christ does not result from a change, conversion, or equation of the substance of the natures . . . but in the incarnate Christ there are and remain two complete, different, distinct natures, the divine and the human, so that according to the deity Christ is and remains of the same substance (*homoousios*) with the Father, but according to the humanity He forever is and remains of the same substance with His brothers."

6. Rainer Maria Rilke, "The Raising of Lazarus," my translation.

7. Leo Tolstoy (Richard Pevear and Larissa Volokhonsky, trans.), *War and Peace* (New York: Alfred A. Knopf, 2007), 986.

8. See Orlando Figes, "Tolstoy's Real Hero" in *The New York Review of Books* 54, no. 18 (22 November 2007).

9. Fyodor Dostoevsky (Richard Pevear and Larissa Volokhonsky, trans.), *The Brothers Karamazov* (New York: Farrar, Straus and Giroux, 2002 edition), 77.

10. AE 17:220–21.

Chapter 6

1. Rainer Maria Rilke, "A Book for the Hours of Prayer," my translation.

2. Abraham Heschel, *Man Is Not Alone: A Philosophy of Religion* (New York: Harper & Row, 1951), 69.

3. Eugene Peterson, *Conversations: The Message with Its Translator* (Colorado Springs, CO: NavPress, 2002), 444.

4. José Ortega Y Gasset, *Meditations on Don Quixote* (New York: W.W. Norton & Co., Inc., 1963), 74.

5. John Gardner. *On Moral Fiction* (San Francisco: Basic Books, 1978), 34.

6. Steven Pressfield. *Gates of Fire: An Epic Novel of the Battle of Thermopylae* (New York: Bantam Books, 2005), i.

7. Eugene Peterson, *First and Second Samuel*, 144–45, quoted in *Conversations: The Message with Its Translator* (Colorado Springs: NavPress Publishing Group, 2007), 444.

8. See, for example, Walter Von Loewenich, *Luther's Theology of the Cross*, trans. Herbert Bouman (Minneapolis: Augsburg, 1982).

Epilogue

1. St. Ephraim Syrus, "On the Death of a Child: Motives for Restraining Sorrow," *Selected Metrical Hymns and Homilies* (London: Robert B. Blackader, 1853).